Empire Mil

Alan Duckworth

Ashleigh Barrow Books

ISBN 978 0 952217381

Copyright © Alan Duckworth

No part of this book may be reproduced, or stored in, or introduced into a retrieval system, or transmitted in any form, or by any means, without prior permission of the publisher.

Ashleigh Barrow Books
Leyland

Cover illustration by Heather Dickinson

Prologue

They'd meandered up dusty Brokenstone Road to Step Back and then followed sheep tracks to the buttresses by Ogden Force.

It was a fiery June day. Maybe the cold rush of water and the shade of the buttresses had drawn them. They sat on the boulders at the river's side; Ben Preston, aged ten, his face, bare arms and legs already reddened; his sister Maria, a half-timer at Empire Mill; Mick Moon and his sister Mary, also half-timers; 'Smithy', ten like Ben, and still at the Board School; the twins, two eight year old boys; and little Sadie O'Donnell, only ten, but who had given up school to help on her mother's fruit stall, boiling oranges to make them bigger.

They were all more or less in rags, hand-me-downs from bigger brothers and sisters. All in clogs, except Sadie, who went bare-foot everywhere.

Exquisite dragonflies were suspended where the water was still and deep and where a keen eye might distinguish a brown, speckled trout suddenly stand out against the brown, speckled river bed. Above them the buttresses, on either side of the stream, confronted one another like bare-knuckle fighters, their jutting granite jaws barely six feet apart. This was 'Lovers' Leap,' a traditional 'dare', and the source of the deep foreboding in Ben's breast. He sat cross-legged, his bony knees emerging from ragged, corduroy trousers. His fingers twined and untwined snatches of tough moorland grass.

He couldn't enjoy the day or the fine vistas. The idiotic brawling of the twins distracted him. Mick Moon's serene contempt ignited a blaze of anger in his breast, and then there was the proximity of Sadie, the prettiest girl in Over Darren, whom he'd loved with the whole of his honest little heart since he'd been five years old.

"I know you daredn't do it," Mick said again.

"Who says I want to?" Ben demanded, his voice all shaky.

Mick had his fingers hooked round his grimy knees. He was big for his age, rangy, with a broad, high-cheekboned face. He tossed his head to clear the fair hair out of his eyes.

"Peas hot, peas hot, peas hot, full of snot," the twins began chanting.

Ben's Mum, Sally-Anne had a pie and pea shop in Back Hacking Street and when business was slack she'd send Ben out with a canister of hot peas to sell door-to-door. He was supposed to shout, 'peas hot, peas hot,' as he went along, but with a deeply ingrained horror of drawing attention to himself, he would merely mumble it.

"How are folk supposed to know you're there?" Sally-Anne demanded. "Shout lad, shout!"

And so, with a flaming face he would shout 'peas hot, peas hot' in a quivery falsetto, until he was out of her earshot, when he would revert to a mumble. The whole thing was an ordeal. The canister was heavy and hot and the wire handle dug into his fingers, so he had to keep changing hands.

Local kids had been quick to spot his predicament and would

follow him, chanting 'peas hot, peas hot, full of snot.' Shaming as it was, it would alert people, and doors along the street would open and he'd sell a few pennorth, lightening his load.

He knew he should punish the twins, but knew from experience that, though younger, they were tough and fought fiercely. Only extreme violence of a kind Ben was incapable of would quell them. He glared at them and they hooted their derision.

"Shut up you two," Mick ordered. "What about it Ben?"

Ben said nothing, just swallowed hard.

"What about you Smithy?"

Smithy wiped his shirt sleeve across his nose. "I'm not blooming daft," he said with lugubrious indignation.

"You are Smithy," Mick said pleasantly.

"Well not that daft," he said darkly and began to scuff the rock with the heel of his clog.

"It's up to you then Ben," Mick said.

"He's too soft," Mary said scornfully.

"He's not soft," Maria said. "Show'em our Ben."

"Show us, Ben," Mick echoed.

All eyes were on him. He couldn't bear it. He couldn't bear that Sadie was witnessing his humiliation. He stared at the ground and willed it to open and swallow him up.

"I haven't seen you do it," he mumbled.

"You will, if Sadie asks me," Mick replied.

Sadie had a helmet of blue/black hair. Her complexion was high-coloured and her eyes were huge and dark brown and as merry as the stream that ran by. She looked horrified.

"I can't. I can't. You might get hurt."

"I won't."

"Oh no."

She smiled and her colour and her dimples deepened. She looked at the other girls.

"Go on," they shrilled excitedly.

"Have I to?"

"Yes," they shrilled again.

"All right, do it." She gave him a mock glare and then screwed up her eyes at the enormity of it.

Mick sprang to his feet and climbed up round the back of the buttresses. He appeared above them, his silhouette quite black against the white-gold sky. He measured the distance with his eye, took a few steps back from the edge. Sadie held her face. It was full of horror, but her eyes were bright with excitement.

Mick waited until mind and body were focused, until the suspense down below was unbearable, then exploded, powered forward, leapt into the air, seemingly suspended there for a second, before landing at the very edge of the far buttress. He landed with a flourish, the irons of his clogs striking a shower of sparks on the rough granite.

"Mick!" Sadie gasped, when he sauntered back into view, hands in pockets.

"It's easy. Come on 'Peas Hot,' your turn."

Ben didn't budge.

"Will you do it, if Sadie asks you?" Maria asked slyly.

"Course."

"Go on Sadie," they shrilled again.

Sadie bit her lip, then nodded.

For Ben it was a death sentence, but he had no choice now. He would rather die than have Sadie think him a coward. He stood up. His heart pounded so, it shook his whole body. The blood roared in his ears until he could hear nothing. Although his eyes still functioned, it was the internal images of imminent catastrophe that prevailed.

His clogs skittered on the granite. He kicked them off and the hot stone burned his soles, calloused as they were from going bare-foot on the flags at home and in the yard. He edged towards the leap and gauged it against the limits of his ability. He couldn't do it. He knew it was beyond him.

Down below, upturned faces squinted against the sun. He took a last look at Sadie. She was shielding her eyes with her palm. The inside of her arm was quite white. He stepped back a few paces, gripped the granite with his bare toes, noticed how grubby his feet were. 'Get it over with,' he thought to himself, ran at it, and launched himself...

The sun burned right through his thin black body and flailing arms, until for a moment he disappeared.

The water rushed at him, black and icy. It was sluggish, thickened with mud and other viscous stuff. Holding his rifle clear and propelled by the weight on his back, Ben couldn't avoid coming up against the crater's other occupant, a dead comrade.
A star shell burst over no man's land, lit up the German line, turned water and mud to silver for a second, then the pre-dawn blackness jumped back. The body revolved in the water, disturbed by Ben's movement. Although the head was featureless, although there was no discernable mouth, it spoke:
'They haven't cut the wire. They haven't cut the wire.'
Then the German machine guns came back to the job in hand, painstakingly, obsessively, compulsively. For every dozen rounds that kicked up the mud or made blue sparks fly from the barbed wire, one would find a home in flesh and bone and another man would falter.
Ben struggled from the dead man's maudlin embrace, and climbed out of the shell hole. He joined the thinning line of his comrades, still going forward.

Chapter One

Built on the southern heights, Empire Mill dominated Over Darren, only the Jubilee Tower on the moors overtopped it. By day, its weaving sheds were ramparts of smoked red brick. By night they were black cliffs perforated by panoramas of light. In the Italianate style that was popular in the mid 19th century, its chimney was a 300 foot high brick campanile that most days flew a black banner of smoke. The materials of Empire Mill's construction were the finest. No economies had been made. Even the coal stores and stables were lined with first quality bricks. The five vast weaving sheds had floors of English oak. The five storey block of offices had roofs of Lakeland slate. Machine shops, store rooms, warehouses had the best fittings and equipment money could buy. It had been the pinnacle of cotton magnate Enoch Shorrock's achievement, his grand design, his legacy, and it had bankrupted him.

His timing had been bad. Empire Mill had been conceived of and commenced in the late 1850s. By the time it was ready the American Civil War was raging and there was no cotton. The huge weaving sheds remained empty. The giant steam engines remained motionless. When trade picked up, it was too late for Enoch. He was a broken man, having been the first man in the town, first Chairman of the Local Board, first Mayor of the Borough, first freeman of the town. Although he ended his life in poverty, whenever he looked up and saw Empire Mill on the skyline he felt a thrill of pride. He had built it. His energy, ambition, and vision had created it. It was his monument, a cathedral among the churches and chapels of lesser mills. Long after he was dead it would stand and men would marvel.

Jack Shaw was the owner now, a more cautious man, a man who kept his affairs close, a man who had made his fortune, but affected the manners and appearance of an ordinary worker, much to the annoyance of his wife Esther, who had aspirations.

Jack and his son Perry arrived every morning at seven, driven in their motorcar by the chauffeur Dickens. They paused at the gatekeepers lodge.

"Any locked out this morning Ephraim?" Jack asked.

"Not a one, Mr. Shaw."

Work started at 6.00 and at fifteen minutes past the gate was locked and any latecomers missed a day's work. Jack and Perry parted company when the car stopped. Perry went to the office block and Jack entered the weaving shed with its roar of a thousand looms. It was a noise that would have daunted some, but Jack didn't flinch. Like many his hearing had suffered over the years, but he was adept at lip-reading and exchanged greetings with many of the hands. Most of the men wore singlets, light trousers and were bare-footed, safer on the oil-impregnated floor. The women had long, black dresses and plain blouses.

Jack walked through each shed in turn, then the winding department, the warehouses, the machine shops, the stores, the goods inward and goods outward, unloading and loading bays, and then crossed the mill-yard to the offices. He had no office of his own, not even a desk. He walked into the manager's office as usual without knocking.

"Everything in order Eddie?"

Eddie Moy was a stout, florid man, who in the July heat would have been more comfortable in his shirt sleeves, but he persevered with his dark jacket and mopped his corrugated brow with a handkerchief instead.

"All in order Jack."

Jack, by his expression, begged to differ.

"The looms on that Dewhirst order are all stopped. They say they're waiting for weft."

Eddie was about to explain, but Jack cut him off.

"And there's not enough tension on the back threads on those fancy twills."

Eddie opened his mouth again. A spasm of indignation prompted him to snap back, but Jack had gone. He refolded his hankie, mopped his brow again and heaved himself out of his chair.

Jack went through the counting house where all was suddenly silent and rows of heads were bent industriously over their ledgers.

It was said that the foundation stone for Empire Mill's chimney was the largest block of stone ever quarried. No way of ascertaining that now, as nine tenths of it was buried. Jack passed it and glanced up at the towering chimney. It made his head swim and his heart race. He got a firm hold of the rail and went down into the boiler room. Two, three-flued Lancashire boilers, the size of houses, roared away. He exchanged a few words with Boilerhouse Bill, a huge fellow with hands like shovels and then descended more steps to the engine house.

It was well-lit with electric lamps. The light reflected on the brass, copper and oiled steel of two horizontal cross-compound steam engines. Brass rails guarded them and brass name plates on their cylinder heads identified them as Beatrice and Louise. The governors whirled and the mighty travel of the flywheels made the drive ropes hum and the very air vibrate. Jack hesitated at the edge of the floor of highly polished oak blocks.

Empire Mill's engine tenter, Cuthbert Bell appeared out of the shadows, his polishing cloth in his hand. He was in his seventies, but hale enough with a full head of hair, albeit white now.

"Can I come in Cuthbert?"

"Aye, but you must take off your clogs."

Jack stood and watched the engines for a moment, admired the smooth flexing of steel sinews, the energetic rhythm of the pistons, then followed Cuthbert into his workshop where they sat by the bench. Cuthbert pushed his tobacco pouch over.

"Owt new?" Cuthbert asked when they'd both got their pipes going.

"I've bought an island."

Cuthbert refused to react. They puffed in silence for a moment, then he said:

"That'll be Esther."

"Aye, well old Enoch had one, so we have to."

"It'll keep her out of mischief."

"It will. There's a big house for her to furnish."

"You've got a big house."

"Aye well that might be needed for summat else soon. When this war starts, it'll make a grand hospital."

"It's coming then?" Cuthbert said.

"Aye it's coming."

"You'll make a bob or two."

"There'll be uniforms and bandages wanted right enough, but it'll need a canny head. There's plenty of competition."

"There's not so many cannier than thee."

"I'll not be around for ever."

"They say it'll be over by Christmas. You'll last that long."

Jack sucked the stem of his pipe and said nothing. Cuthbert meditated this for a moment and then followed a line of thought.

"Your Nathaniel's a captain in the Territorials. He'll have to do more than pose in his uniform now."

Jack pulled a face.

"Don't worry about him. He'll see himself right. He's courting Lord Hoddersdale's lass, who's well in with the War Office top brass, so he should be able to land a cushy staff officer's job for our Nathanial."

"Then there's your Perry."

Jack took out his pipe.

"What do you mean?"

"He'll not want to miss out."

"He's needed here. I've told you I'll not be around for ever."

Cuthbert puffed away for a while.

"Is there summat you're not saying, Jack?"

"I've not been feeling so good, lad, not so clever at all."

"You want to get to t'doctor."

Jack snorted.

"I don't need them to hurry me on my way. Anyway how's that grandson of yours doing in the counting house? Is it suiting him?"

"Better than t'weaving shed that's for sure, but I can't make moss nor sand of him."

"Do you want me to do owt for him?"

"No, leave him there. He'll make summat of himself one day, but I'm beggared if I know what."

Jack eased himself to his feet.

"I'll best be going."

Cuthbert nodded.

"If we're going to be put on war work, that number two boiler'll need re-lining."

"Aye, we'll get it done during t'wakes week."

Cuthbert watched him climb the steps and saw an old man with not much time left.

Chapter Two

Ever since his fall at Lovers' Leap, it was as though Ben had lost a protective layer, as though he lacked that which in others muted the impact of the glories and horrors of the world. Sally-Anne had often found him stock still in the yard at night, staring up at the swarming stars, or lost in a daze, or she'd catch him suddenly turn and stare, as though he'd seen something.
"What is it?" she would demand.
"Nothing," he would reply.
"Well don't just stare at nothing. It gives folk the willies."
His sensitivity was sharpened by the antics of his father Jimmy, a drinking man first and second, and a bricklayer a poor third. He would work until he had enough for a spree, then disappear. Sally-Anne threw him out at last when Ben was six, and he went to live in Briggs Knowles' henhouse, paying his rent and getting

drinking money by doing odd jobs.

When Ben was at school Jimmy would sometimes appear at the gates, maudlin-drunk, begging Ben to give him a cuddle. Sometimes when Ben was doing his hot pea round, Jimmy would weave into view. Ben would see him off with a few coppers, and when the money was short later, he would confess and Sally-Anne would give him a cuff round the ear and declare he was too soft to live.

His sisters all went weaving at Empire Mill and he followed in their footsteps, but he was not a success. It was the thunderous roar of the looms that undid him. Above the deafening clatter of the thousand looms he could hear other things - the detonation of guns, the dying scream of shells, the crash of mortars and the rattle of machine guns. This defeated his concentration. He was unable to produce the necessary high standard. Faultless pieces were required, or everybody got fined. He was the despair of those trying to teach him, but the secret delight of the sadistic foreman Happy Frank, a misery with a long face, a former regular army NCO, who loved to stand parade ground fashion, legs apart, arms behind his back, observing Ben's fumbling, then he would bawl him out with blistering obscenities, non of which Ben could hear, but their import was not lost upon him.

Mick Moon was at Empire Mill too. He was an apprentice mechanic and studying at the technical school. His sister Mary was there, as were the twins. Smithy was in the stores. Sadie's Mum Rose had had a disabling stroke, which left her without speech, so Sadie ran the fruit stall on her own.

Happy Frank overstepped the mark one day, slapping Ben round the head. Ben's sister Elsie saw him do it and ran down to the engine house in her break to tell her Granddad. Cuthbert had a word with Boiler-house Bill, who dragged Happy Frank out and suspended him by the ankles over the mill-dam for a few minutes, long enough for him to see the error of his ways.

It was evident though that Ben wouldn't make a weaver, so Cuthbert spoke to Jack Shaw and he was transferred to the counting house, where he performed better. Indeed he'd been an apt pupil at the Higher Grade School and Miss Forster, the head teacher had hoped to persuade him to continue his studies. She'd even paid a visit to Sally-Anne to that end, but the two strong-willed women had not got on. Sally-Anne said there was no money for it and that was that. Miss Forster had informed her there were scholarships and bursaries for the needy. Sally-Anne didn't see herself as needy and if Miss Forster had produced a bag of sovereigns from her purse there and then, she would only have flung them back in her face.

The chap on the stool next to him at the long counting house table was Joe Wainwright, a big, serious-looking lad who was studying book-keeping. They became pals and Sam promised to pass on his knowledge. Sam was a keen rambler and lover of nature. The two of them often tramped the moors, talking endlessly, making improbable plans for the future. They decided to have a few days walking in the wakes week's holiday.

The market stayed open till late at night and when he'd finished work and done any jobs required of him by his mother, Ben would go and hover by Sadie's stall.

She was too tender-hearted to actually say it, but her expression, when she caught sight of him, clearly said, 'not you again.' And Ben was well aware of this, and the knowledge made him awkward, but he couldn't keep away. Sadie had grown into a beautiful woman with dark good looks. Her slender neck, revealed now her dark hair was up, was sublime. Her figure was slim, but sturdy, but it was her eyes that were her glory, big, brown, lustrous eyes, full of laughter and mischief. They drew other men than Ben and he knew it. And it was one of these other men that Sadie hoped would not turn up while Ben was there.

The piles of oranges glowed as though they were lit from within. Sadie would serve her customers, exchange pleasantries or cheek and then stand, arms folded, a studiedly neutral expression on her face, neither encouraging, nor discouraging Ben.

"What are you doing in the wake's week?" Ben asked.

"Don't know, nothing much probably."

"Not going to Blackpool then?"
She wrinkled her nose.
"Don't fancy that - a lot of silly girls up to no good."
"Our Carrie and Maria are going."
"Oh I didn't mean..."
"No, you're right," Ben said. "It describes them two to a T."
There was silence, then Ben said.
"I'm going walking with Joe Wainwright."
Sadie nodded approvingly.
"That's good. I'm glad. Keep away from the buttresses though," she added with a dazzling smile of mischief.

Ben grinned sheepishly, still embarrassed after seven years. Sadie felt some embarrassment too, and compromised. Ben had recovered well from the fall, but she still felt guilty, felt she somehow owed him something.

Although in his heart Ben knew it was hopeless, he plunged in anyway.

"Look, I'll be back from walking later in the week. Why don't we have a day together?"

Sadie spread her arms and opened wide her eyes.
"I don't know what I'm doing. I just don't know."
"We could have a trip, not Blackpool, but Southport or St Annes."
Sadie shrugged and said nothing.
"Say you'll think about it."
"All right, all right, I'll think about it, but you'd better go, you're putting my customers off."

And Ben had to be content with that.

Chapter Three

In summer the skylights of the weaving sheds at Empire Mill were whitewashed, even so, when the sun shone, temperatures climbed into the nineties and higher. There was a lot of sunshine in the summer of 1914. All the doors to the outside stood open and when they could, the hands would pause for a minute to look out, look up longingly towards the glowing moors, where cool breezes blew.

Jack Shaw stayed at the mill until the workers had gone. Sometimes he stood at the window of the top floor office to watch them, the drab mass of them, women with shawls, men with flat caps or battered bowlers, their clogs thundering over the mill-yard cobbles - the Over Darren artillery.

Sometimes he would point to one.

"We're not working them hard enough; look at that bugger. He's still got enough energy to run."

And nobody knew whether he was joking or not. It was a fact that some of the younger men, even after a full day in the mill, would take a ball on to the mill fields for a kick-about.

Jack liked to walk though the sheds when they were silent and empty. There was a lot to spot: which of the tacklers kept an untidy bench; who didn't clean his tools; whose looms were not being maintained properly.

But the silence, the stillness, the solitude, where only minutes earlier there had been unimaginable aural mayhem and frantic activity, made him reflective. It was like being on the field when the battle's over. The silence, stillness and solitude seemed even more poignant on the last working day in July 1914. It was the commencement of the annual wakes week holiday, when all the mills, all the foundries, all the engineering works, all the quarries and pits closed. Most shops closed too. The market closed, and even the Town Hall closed for a couple of days.

Not everybody was off work. The week was a good opportunity for maintenance and repairs, and already the steam lorry from Foster Yates and Thom was in the mill yard. They'd come to start re-lining the boiler. Jack's son Perry was there, much taller than Jack and impeccably dark suited, but with the same, shrewd intelligent expression. Tall as Perry was, he was dwarfed at the side of Boilerhouse Bill. Jack was more than happy to linger and overlook the preliminaries. He didn't want to get back home too soon, not until the Reverend Pomfret had left.

Reverend Pomfret was vicar of St Jude's, the new church built to serve the spiritual needs of Empire Mill's workers. He'd been the son of a gamekeeper and had grown up observing the life of a big estate, seen the comings and goings of the wealthy, of influential people, society people and had determined that one day he would move in such circles, would be on friendly terms with lords and ladies, would shoot and hunt and enjoy the life of a country gentleman. He was a big, well set-up man, with a leonine head of golden hair and whiskers. He had a deep, melodious voice and was an astute flatterer. He knew how to charm the ladies. On arrival at

Over Darren, he had first ingratiated himself with Thomas and Jane Holden, the town's leading drapers. When Thomas had died suddenly, there was talk of him marrying his widow, but by then Pomfret had the Shaws in his sights and Jane became his housekeeper.

Pomfret made overtures to Jack, but it didn't take him long to realise he'd make no progress there, so took another tack. It was a vicar's accepted right, nay duty, to call on his wealthier parishioners and take tea. He was soon a regular visitor in Esther Shaw's drawing room. Esther was an easy conquest.

Esther's origins were no more elevated than Jack's. Most Monday mornings her mother had had to pawn the family's Sunday best to see them through till payday Friday, but young Esther had insulated herself from reality by living in a dream world, a world of princesses and princes, castles and romance. She'd married Jack when he was no more than a thrifty, hard-working, weaving-shed manager, thinking her dreams would always be just that - dreams, but when they began to do well, when they began to go up in the world, when they got a villa in the leafy part of town, when they got a servant, then she began to think her dreams could come true.

Her pregnancies and labours had all been difficult and when Evelyn, the last, was born, Esther assumed the trappings of an invalid and eschewed the rough manners of Over Darren and planned an altogether different way of life. Pomfret encouraged her.

When their car rolled up outside Woodlands, Jack was glad to see Pomfret's pony and trap had gone. His relief was to be short-lived however.

Woodlands had been another of Enoch Shorrock's flights of fantasy. There had been a substantial villa here for many years, but Enoch had embellished and extended it, dwarfed it with a three storey Elizabethan facade, complete with battlements, and added a huge conservatory with an Italian mosaic floor. There were 20 bedrooms, not counting servants' rooms, three receiving rooms, a formal dining room and a family dining room, morning room, great hall, library, games room, studies, school room, nursery, gun and trophy room. Outside were hot houses, ice houses, stables, garage, workshops, chauffeur's and gardeners' cottages.

The great hall lived up to its name, but a massive fireplace set its lofty dimensions at naught. It was a fireplace of spectacular ornateness, ornateness that was little short of being nightmarish. Its stone and mahogany, its beaten brass and marble were carved and sculpted into flora and fauna, into fiendish designs and flourishes. No fire that burned there could ever look anything but meagre, so none was ever lit.

Esther was in her receiving room, a fussy room full of flounces and drapes. Every surface was covered with embroidered linen and ponderous ornaments. There were chaises and sofas and tables and upholstered footstools of every size and shape. Evelyn was keeping her mother company.

The two women could not have been more different. Evelyn was thin, erect and severe. She knew she was plain and cross-looking. She knew that any young man who paid her attention had his eyes on Jack's money, not on her charms. She was resigned to spinsterhood.

Esther was horizontal, shapeless, powdered and rouged. Evelyn was simply, starkly dressed in plain white blouse and black skirt, her hair dragged back from her pale brow. Esther was all frills and lace in pastel shades, her hair elaborately coiffeured and sculpted. Yet many would have seen that they were mother and daughter at once, and those that did not, would not have been surprised to learn the fact.

"Jack, Jack. Where have you been? You've missed Reverend Pomfret," Esther complained.

Jack seemed to bear the disappointment pretty well. He rubbed his hands.

"Have you rung for dinner? It's steak pudding."

"Always thinking of your stomach! Good news though; the Reverend Pomfret has agreed to accompany us to Scotland."

Jack's face turned to thunder, an expression that could quell the most belligerent trade union man, but which had no effect on Esther.

Perry, who had followed his father into the room, put an arm round his shoulders and squeezed.

"Isn't that good news Father?"

Even Evelyn, so fiercely erect, could not suppress a smile.

"I'm not having that pompous windbag..."

Esther cut him off.

"Don't be silly, with Perry not coming, the Reverend will be a great help, especially so if Nathanial lets us down too. Oh here he is."

Nathanial sauntered in. He was Perry's younger brother all right, but much of the strength and character of the older man was missing. Handsome he was, but in a way that was insubstantial compared to his brother's rugged looks. The lines of his face were finer; his features more delicately drawn, but weaker. The light-coloured summer suit he sported only emphasised his lack of substance.

"Nathanial," his Mother exclaimed. "Are you coming to Scotland? Have you decided?"

"I have Mother and I'm afraid it's no. Something's cropped up."

"That settles it then. We can't possibly manage without the Reverend Pomfret."

Nathanial took an orange out of his pocket and began to peel it.

"Don't eat that. You dinner's ready," Esther complained.

"My dear Mother, it'll take more than an orange to satisfy me, a momentary sweetness, then it's gone, forgotten, finished with."

He dug his finely manicured fingers into the fruit and began to strip it. The room filled with the scent of oranges.

Chapter Four

Wakes week was a time to escape, to try out a different sort of life, to experience fleetingly, and in a very dilute form, the lifestyle of the idle rich. Originally based on local fairs, when working folk would have one or two unofficial days off without pay, it had by 1914 become an established week's holiday, though still without pay. With the growth of the railways travel had become possible for ordinary workers.

Special trains ran from Over Darren Station to Blackpool, Morecambe and north Wales, to Scarborough and Bridlington. It seemed like the whole town was being mobilised. The station was thronged and there were long queues at all the ticket barriers. Steam engines, distant cousins to Empire Mill's Louise and Beatrice, bellowed and steam clouds billowed, causing infants to wail.

Thousands were setting off, seeking a break, a rest, fun and games, an adventure, but above all the opportunity to see the world differently, to get away from the grim, gritty grind of work and sleep. To that they would have to return, and with an awareness of what life might have been, if they'd been born into more comfortable circumstances, but for now a week stretched before them. In 1914 they would not in fact return to the life they had known, and, maybe knowing this, the kind old sun put on a bit of a show, shining bountifully, letting them make the most of it.

Ben and Sam did not take the train. They boarded a tram and travelled to Blackburn and the town's northern terminus at Wilpshire, on the doorstep of the Ribble Valley, where they were to camp and tramp for a few days. They had no tent, just a blanket each, bread and cheese and a bottle of ginger beer.

The tram was full of day-trippers in their summer finery, and Ben and Sam were glad to get off and put some distance between themselves and the crowds. Cyclists passed them in ones and twos and sometimes in a flock. They marched on until they passed the last of the big villa residences and had an uninterrupted view of the Sphynx-like Pendle Hill, its golden flanks shimmering in the heat.

They'd stuffed their jackets in their haversacks and were striding along in shirt sleeves, rolled up.

Sam was completely immersed in the adventure, consulting his map and calculating how far they could walk and where would be a good place to spend the night. Ben was divided. A part of him was upset at leaving Sadie. What if, by his absence, he missed an opportunity? Shouldn't he have been more forceful about spending time with her? What if, because he wasn't there she encouraged someone else? Thus did he torment himself, when all the glories of an English summer morning were set out around him.

By mid-morning their sandwiches and ginger beer were gone. They tramped past the new St Mary's asylum at Whalley and reached Mitton. The sun found gold, flashing on spears of it in the grass, winking on medallions in the foliage, but green predominated, not the fresh, almost startling green of May, but a mellow green, a green that was patched here and there by a darker green of fields of crops, or a lighter green, almost yellow, where fields had been mown. There was bird-song and the distant voices of farm workers.

Venerable Mitton Church looked like it had grown there. Its graveyard, with stones fleeced with yellow and lime lichen, promised a death that was no more than a prolonged slumber in a warm and friendly field. Here they passed into Yorkshire.

They rested on the parapet of an old stone bridge. The river rolled by unhurriedly below. Sam looked at his map.

"It's the Hodder. Why don't we follow it to its source?"

"How far is it?"

"Dunno, but we've got all week."

"No, I need to be back by Thursday." Ben said, rubbing his finger on the rough stone.

"Why?"

"I've got things to do."

"What?"

Ben didn't answer, but led the way off the bridge down to the path by the river. He'd already decided he'd made a big mistake, that he should be with Sadie. What could she possibly be doing on her own all week? Up to no good, he was sure of it.

Jack Shaw and his party had a compartment to themselves in the train travelling north. Jack had woken feeling dislocated, distant, as though everything was remote, as though he was viewing everything through the wrong end of a telescope. It meant though that the Reverend Pomfret's pronouncements were easier to ignore. There were four of them. Esther and Evelyn were the others.

At Glasgow they changed trains. They passed over the Clyde with its shipyards. The second city of Empire had some noble buildings and some mean ones too. They emerged from it at last and picked up speed heading for the Highlands.

Lochs and Bens abounded. Waterfalls dropped from distant crags. Troops of red deer, hardly visible against the red bracken, crossed the glens. Pine trees proliferated, and only the lightest clouds, mere wisps, the merest white feathers, drifted their shadows over the mountain contours, and cast white amongst the shimmering blue of the lakes.

Jack was used to viewing landscapes with an eye to economic possibilities, estimating its value per acre, but in his enfeebled condition he saw it differently, saw it for what it was, saw it had a value beyond its price, beyond any price. It soothed him and soon he slept.

The Reverend Pomfret, sitting diagonally opposite, bent forward and drew Esther's attention to the sleeping old man.

"I do hope the journey doesn't prove too much for him," he whispered.

Esther scrutinised her husband in a way she'd not done for some time. She noticed how shrunken his face had become, how deep set his eyes and how tremulous his jaw.

"You don't think he's ill?"

The Reverend Pomfret's face bore an expression of sympathy that suggested he rather feared so.

"Have you not observed how slow his movements have become, how short his breath?"

"He's never said a word," Esther protested.

Evelyn lay down her copy of *Militant Woman*.

"He won't do and he won't see a doctor either. He's scared."

"Scared!" exclaimed Esther, who had never heard the word associated with Jack Shaw.

"We must take good care of him. He's dear to us all," the Reverend observed.

"We should take some of the work of running Empire Mill off him," Evelyn said. "I'm happy to do my share."

Reverend Pomfret rewarded her with a smile such as one would bestow on a child, who makes an absurd but noble vow. Evelyn took his meaning, responded with a glare and picked up her book.

The sleep did Jack good. He awoke when they pulled into the station at Mallaig and he supervised the unloading of the luggage, frustrating Reverend Pomfret's attempts to treat him like an invalid. On board the steamer, Shiel, he made himself known to the Captain and was invited to inspect the engine.

They got their first glimpse of Cara as the sun was setting behind it. The sea was like smoked silk, with here and there glittering highlights that were quite dazzling. Cara's profile was dark blue against a white gold sky. As they approached the stone harbour the steamer's engine was throttled back, and when they'd manoeuvred alongside the jetty, was cut altogether. The silence was immense. Such a silence as they'd not experienced in a long time. A lamb's bleat from the distant hills pierced it.

On an eminence above the pine trees they could see the rose coloured granite of Achaglass House, home of the Laird of Cara.

On the jetty a knot of islanders had congregated to greet them.

"I hadn't expected this," Jack Shaw said.

"You're the new Laird," the Captain explained. "You've the power of life or death over them, well the power to make them miserable or happy anyway. They're keen to make a good impression and keener still to see what kind of man you are."

Accustomed as he was to having folk dependant on him for their livelihood, this was something new. He felt humbled.

"They've nowt to fear from me."

Looming up behind him was the Reverend Pomfret and the glitter in his eye as he surveyed isle and islanders hinted at a different sentiment altogether. Was this to be the country gentleman's estate he'd always dreamed of?

Chapter Five

The path left the river and climbed up into the trees. Here the sun's bounty was restricted to golden dapples on the forest floor. Oak and sycamore, elm and beech were still, drowsing in the mid-day heat. The only sound was bird-song and the excited chatter of the river down below.

They emerged from tree cover to a dusty road, with a bridge and an inn.

"Let's get a drink," Sam said in the voice of a man with a prodigious thirst.

"Ginger beer for me," Ben said.

"Ginger beer! Have a pint."

"I don't drink."

"I don't drink," Sam said indignantly, "not what you call drinking, but on a day like this…"

"Ginger beer," Ben insisted.

Sam was about to argue further, but remembered who Ben's father was and said no more.

It was cool inside. The inn's walls were thick enough to keep out the heat and the floors were stone flagged. There was a fair crowd of ramblers at the bar, but the landlord, bald, snub-nosed, with bushy eyebrows, was not to be hurried. He served everyone with slow deliberation, making appropriate remarks about the weather.

Ben and Sam took their drinks into a snug, where there were old settles worn smooth by generations of fustian-clothed backsides.

"This is the life," Sam declared, after taking a long drink. He regarded with satisfaction the creamy froth that clung to the sides of the glass. "Think what we'd normally be doing, heads down over dusty order books with old Barker's beady eye on us."

Ben stared at his glass. The ginger beer was grey with a white effervescing head. Beads of condensation stood on the glass. He said nothing, but thought at least he'd be nearer Sadie. Sam allowed the silence to continue for a while, before saying.

"Is there something on your mind?"

Ben was about to deny it, but then thought there'd be some relief in talking about it, so admitted he was missing Sadie.

Sam frowned.

"Is there anything agreed between you two?"

"No, not exactly. I can't bring her to it, but we've been sweet on each other since childhood."

Sam had heard the gossip about Nathanial Shaw hanging around Sadie's fruit stall. Everybody had, apart from Ben. Many had seen the two of them together; Nathanial's bright blue Hispano-Suiza tourer wasn't exactly inconspicuous.

"I should try and put it out of your mind old chap. Make the most of now. The future can take care of itself, without you having to worry."

Ben nodded, but didn't look convinced. His dark, moody looks remained unchanged.

When the pub was quieter, the landlord came round collecting glasses.

"Where you heading, lads?"

"Up river, to the source," Sam said.

"That's Lord Hoddersdale's land," the landlord pointed out. "He owns most of the county around here."

"He won't mind if we walk on a bit of it then, will he?" Sam reasoned.

The landlord looked doubtful.

"You want to watch out for his gamekeepers. They shoot first and ask questions afterwards."

"We're not poachers."

"They don't always take the trouble to find that out. I'd go somewhere else if I were you. Strangers don't find a big welcome up there."

"Maybe he's right," Ben said, after he'd left.

"Rubbish. We've a right to walk where we want."

Ben said no more, but his doubts were not stilled.

Each wing of Hoddersdale Hall was like a mansion in itself. They stood forward of the main body of the hall, and in the space between was an ornamental lake and a fountain, which was usually switched off, as its 70 foot jet soaked visitors. It soaked the gardeners too, though they were of less account.

It was built of red brick. Armies of brick makers and brick layers must have been employed, and an army of servants was employed now. Long before the sun rose to illuminate the grand front elevation, there were lights in the house, as maids lit fires and hustled hither and thither with jugs of hot water, valets polished boots and brushed coats, and in the kitchen the housekeeper, butler, cook, under-butlers and assistant-cooks planned that day's campaign.

And long after the sun had flushed the rear of the hall in rose tints and flashed signals off the hundreds of windows, long after it set and all was in darkness, lights were on as sewing maids stitched dresses, torn in the ballroom; housemaids cleared the aftermath of dinner parties; and scullery maids tackled the dirty dishes that stood in piles on every surface in the vast kitchen.

It was Ralph Bradshaw, the 4th Lord Hoddersdale, who had had the hall built in the 1740s when his star had blazed high in the constellation of English nobility. George II and Henry Pelham, the Prime Minister, were frequent guests. The Bradley family owed their fortune and eminence to their ancestor, Sir Percy de Bradley, who had been an enthusiastic and ruthless servant in William the Conqueror's crushing of the North, slaying Saxons and seizing their lands. He had been rewarded with vast territories.

Nine hundred years later the Bradleys still owned much of the land. The seventh Earl, Stanley Bradley, after Eton and Oxford had entered the army, and after service in South Africa against the Boers, had become a Chief of the Staff College and had retired as Brigadier General. He was a small man, but hard as flint, unsmiling, unflappable, and unshaken in his conviction that he was a superior being.

The conviction was shared by his son and three daughters and by his wife, Elizabeth, who was if anything more stiff-backed and haughty than he was. It was the youngest girl, the plainest, Caroline who was engaged to Nathanial Shaw. She had a healthy, outdoor freshness. She was frank and freckled, open, almost naive, but much the pleasantest of the three girls. The others, Geraldine and Gertrude were exquisite beauties in shimmering silk, hotly pursued by young men of noble blood. The son, Rupert, was a captain in the Royal Horse Guards, a keen sportsman and hunter, thought of by all who knew him as 'a splendid chap.'

With war imminent, Stanley Bradley had come out of retirement and was busy supervising the raising of battalions from the industrial towns of the county. Hoddersdale Hall had not been so busy for years. It came into its own. Like a dark star it drew all towards it, all the resources, all the wealth, all the people, some seeking jobs, some seeking preferment, some willingly, some unwillingly. In the former category, but soon to be in the latter, were Ben and Sam.

The squat, be-whiskered head had watched them haughtily, its fur wet and spiky, its sinuous brown body poised. It paused long enough to satisfy its curiosity and then returned to the river. A ripple betrayed its presence for a few moments and then that too was gone.

"An otter!" Sam declared. They both felt honoured by the creature's attention, privileged to glimpse its world.

They had got the attention of other creatures too, coming up though the wood. Hares had peered round bushes before zigzagging away; deer had regarded them with stupefied astonishment for a second, before bounding off; and whenever they came into clearings, kestrals and buzzards were hanging aloft, carrying out observations.

"Look at all this," Sam said. "And how many folk down in Over Darren even know it's here?"

Ben didn't answer. He felt others were watching, other creatures, that the very trees bristled with outrage at their intrusion.

"How can anybody own all this?" Sam demanded. "How can they own a river? Do they own the water? Do they own the rain? Do they own the air? Do we need permission to breathe?"

They came to a stone village and tried unsuccessfully to get refreshment. At the inn they met with nothing but hostility. Backs were turned. Cold shoulders were presented. They tried to buy food at cottages, but met the same response. They might have been enemy troops in an occupied land, among people scared of reprisals, if they offered help.

As night fell, they were still going up-river, looking for somewhere to camp. They found a grassy hollow at the river's edge, well screened by trees. While it was still light Sam examined the map.

"Well we're going to starve at this rate. There's nowhere to go except Hoddersdale Hall and I don't think we'd get much hospitality there."

"Well there's plenty of water," Ben said kneeling on the bank, scooping up handfuls, "and there's fish."

"Fish!" Sam exclaimed and scrambled over to peer over his shoulder. "Fish! I've got matches. There's plenty of twigs in the woods back there."

"You've got to catch one first."

The brown trout turned lazily this way and that, seemingly within easy reach in the clear water.

"It shouldn't be difficult, just needs a bit of patience," Sam said and lay face down on the bank.

It was dark all around by now. Only the river retained some light, some afterglow of the bright day. So intent were they that they never heard the men creep up behind them, men with stout cudgels, men who struck without warning.

Two hours, two hours sentry duty. Ben stared out into no man's land. Two hours to stay awake, staring out towards the German line, the high ground, black, against a dark blue, starry sky. The Germans always had the high ground. Two hours to scrutinize the horizon for movement, to peer into the blackness for some shifting shadow that might resolve itself into the shapes of a raiding party. Men often thought there was something, and would let off a round. This would get other sentries going and get the Germans firing back, then everybody would be turned out, cursing and fumbling for their bayonets. And it could be nothing. You might hear a noise from the wire. Was it Germans with wire cutters, or just rats, nosing about among the empty bully beef tins that had been thrown out there? Better to fire though surely, even if it meant a sleepless night, better than having a raiding party in the trench.

One night the Germans sent over a party of big, powerful men, who lifted a sentry bodily out of the trench and spirited him away. Of course he must have been asleep for them to get so close, without him hearing. Fall asleep, and that might happen. Fall asleep, and the Germans might be in the trench. Fall asleep, and you might be shot by your own. Falling asleep on sentry duty was a capital offence. A man in the Lancashire Fusiliers was shot at dawn by firing squad, but they say it was the third time he'd been caught napping.

Ben stared out into no man's land. He was cold and his limbs were stiffening up. He stifled a yawn, relaxed his grip on his rifle, but soon was gripping it as tightly as ever. He stared and he stared, until the whole of no man's land seemed to be swarming with suspicious movement, as though the whole German army were out there, creeping towards him.

Chapter Six

Glasgow seemed to be full of soldiers. They were on the street. They were at the station, on the platforms. They were in the trains. No need for the newspaper placards to scream 'It's War!' The evidence of military upheaval was everywhere to see.

There were soldiers on the move all over Europe, millions of them. The great Russian army was marching westward. The French army was poised to push into Alsace Lorraine. The German army, with enemies on two fronts, needed a quick victory against the French. Their troops were in Belgium already, with only the tiny Belgian army to oppose them.

All over the world troops were being mobilised; from Germany's African colonies; from all corners of the British Empire troops were being recalled. In Canada, Australia and New Zealand young men were volunteering. The Indian army was preparing to sail for

Europe.

War had been expected for years and the plans had long been ready. The British Expeditionary Force, not much bigger than the Belgian army, was on its way to France. Soon it would be all that stood between Germany and victory.

Cara had been a tonic for Jack Shaw. The invigorating breezes, the vast seascapes, with the Western Isles profiled against an unending sky, the salty humour of the locals had done his heart good. The locals too felt cheered. Their fears had been unfounded. Their new English landlord was much like themselves, tough and shrewd. The Reverend Pomfret's preaching had not gone down well however.

The declaration of war had a surprisingly heartening effect on Empire Mill's workforce, when they returned to work after the holiday. The gloomy prospect of a whole year of weaving shed, workshop and counting house, before they could have another holiday, was lightened. They had something else to think about. The future might hold other prospects. This was certainly so for the young men. Excitement beckoned. Escape from the tyranny of the looms beckoned. The chance to go to places they could never have dreamed of seeing beckoned: 'Bugger Blackpool, I'm off to Belgium'.

For the women too, new possibilities dawned. Already there was talk of them being needed in munitions factories, and of higher wages on offer.

On the drive to work on the first morning back, Jack considered the implications. He knew they'd lose workers. He knew there'd be tough negotiations over pay, but what concerned him most was Perry's attitude. Would he realise he was needed at Empire Mill? Would he realise that his work there was more valuable to the country than anything he could do in uniform? Father and son were silent in the car, keeping their thoughts to themselves.

The mill had been silent for over a week. No banner of smoke had fluttered from the 300 foot campanile. Loading bays and delivery bays had been unmanned. Louise and Beatrice had been at rest.

Only in the boiler house had there been activity, but the vastness of the mill rendered the men who worked there insignificant, of no more account than mice in a cathedral.

On the Monday morning, the boilers were fired up. The blue sky was besmirched. The mill engines began to turn under Cuthbert's critical eye. In the weaving sheds the first loom was up and running, setting up a lonely, galloping rhythm in the corner, then others started up and joined the charge. The weavers, who'd been swapping holiday yarns, could no longer hear each other, and had to mime, using gestures and exaggerated lip movements. More looms were up and running, and the weaving shed was rocking with an ear-shattering din that seemed almost palpable, almost as though it were a hostile element that could stifle, injure, annihilate human life.

In the counting house, the clerks were taking down the ledgers, filling the ink wells with different coloured inks, setting out their pens and ebony rulers.

Ben and Sam sported bruises and cuts.

"Had a lovers' tiff?" Reuben, one of the costing clerks, enquired.

Neither was in the mood to answer. They'd been taken by the gamekeepers and kept over-night at Hoddersdale Hall. Sam's vociferous protests had only earned him further bruises. For Ben, what was real and what was not real, what was a dream and what was not, had become confused.

Had the 7th Earl not been absorbed in his war work, he would have taken a personal interest in the red-handed taking of poachers, as it was he waved away the Estate Manager's efforts to convey to him the enormity of the crime. Feeling miffed he retaliated by letting them go.

"Come back on August 12th lads and we'll arrange a warmer welcome," had been his parting shot.

The first Empire Mill man in uniform was Mick Moon. He joined the Royal Field Artillery. As a well-made, good-looking lad, his appearance on the streets of Over Darren made the girls weak at the knees.

Mick and Sadie were old allies. He was the handsomest man in town and she was the most beautiful girl. They had an affinity. They had an understanding of each other. And yet they were not drawn to one another, not attracted in a physical, nor an emotional way. Sadie was one of the first Mick called on in his uniform and he invited her to take a walk in the park.

Sadie's life was, as she put it to herself, complicated. She was glad to have the chance to air the circumstances. She knew she could confide in Mick, knew he was amoral, totally unshockable, and pretty shrewd, so she took down her straw hat from behind the door, shushed her mother's mimed protestations, and took Mick's arm. They headed in the direction of the park.

Bold Venture Park was a favourite resort for Over Darren folk on a Sunday. A band played in the summer months. There was a lake with swans, an aviary, a conservatory, a refreshment kiosk, broad walks and secluded walks.

On such a fine August Sunday the park was thronged. Among the many heading that way were Ben, Sally-Anne and Grandfather Cuthbert. Cuthbert enjoyed critically appraising the bands, having been a cornet player in his youth.

Sadie and Mick stayed away from the crowds round the bandstand. They wanted to talk.

"So what are you doing in uniform?" Sadie asked. "Is it to impress the girls?"

"Just doing my bit for King and country."

She gave him a sidelong, sceptical glance, then squeezed his arm.

"I don't like to think of them shooting at you."

"Oh I can look after myself lass. Trust me for that."

They walked on in silence for a while.

"I've been hearing things about you," Mick said.

"They're all talking about me are they?" Sadie said with indignation.

"Don't flatter yourself, but your carrying-on has been noticed."

"What do they say?"

"What do you think?"

"I can well imagine, but they're wrong. It's not because he's Jack Shaw's lad and worth a lot of money. He's funny and kind and sensitive."

"Not what I've heard."

"He is Mick. He's wonderful to me. He tells me things. He knows so much. He's full of ideas. He writes poetry."

"Poetry! I wouldn't trust a man who writes poetry. I've written a few dirty ditties in my time, but never poetry." Mick shook his head doubtfully.

"I know he thinks a lot about me," Sadie insisted.

Mick squeezed her arm.

"How far has this gone?"

"What do you mean?"

He squeezed her arm again.

"You know."

Sadie sighed.

"We've been all over the place in his car. In the holiday week we had a night at a hotel in Harrogate."

Mick whistled.

"Posh, eh? That's better than a quick one up Shorey Bank. So what's he going to do for you?"

"What do you mean?"

"Well you've obliged him. What do you get out of it?"

"Mick! I'm not a prostitute."

"Nobody says you are, but it's the way of the world isn't it? Nobody does owt for nowt. Why do you think he's engaged to that fancy pants daughter of Lord Muck?"

Sadie pushed out her bottom lip, but remained silent.

"Because she's even richer than he is, that's why." Mick went on. "So you should get something out of it. You're struggling now with your mother the way she is, so he should do summat for you."

"He says he wants to break it off with her and marry me," Sadie said petulantly.

Mick stopped and turned to look at her.

"Sadie, Sadie!" he said reproachfully.

"Well, he might!"

In parks all over the country that Sunday bands were playing military airs and stirring patriotic anthems. Many a young man in Bold Venture Park that afternoon announced to his sweetheart that he was going to join up.

Ben was not one of them. He barely heard the music. He barely registered the crowd. The trees, the grass, the distant glitter of the lake were meaningless patterns to him. He hadn't needed Sally-Anne's nudge to spot Sadie on Mick's arm.

Sally-Anne listened to the band with a sense of smug satisfaction. Her low opinion of Sadie O'Donnell had just been confirmed.

Chapter Seven

Perry had carefully preserved the feather in his pocket book. When he got back to the office, he took it out and laid it on the desk top. It was a fine, white feather. A little ruffled at the quill end, but otherwise immaculately preened. It was a fine, white feather and had been given to him that morning by an immaculately groomed young woman when he was in Manchester, visiting the Cotton Exchange. He'd lifted his hat, thanked her and placed it in his pocket book. She'd curled her lip and stalked away.

He blew gently and the feather stirred. He picked it up and twirled it between thumb and forefinger. It really was a fine, white feather.

Coming home in the train he'd considered the implications. He'd marshalled arguments back and forth, pro and con. Of course she was a silly girl, who didn't know what she was doing. On the other hand her motivation was patriotic, or maybe she had a brother in

France, or a sweetheart and felt others should be doing their bit.

The fact was the army had to be clothed and somebody had to manage the mills that produced the cloth. If the head of every manufacturing concern enlisted, the country would be at a standstill, the war would be lost. And yet, and yet, a beautiful young woman had branded him a coward and he had had no answer, no answer that swept the accusation aside, no answer that would make such a woman blush and apologise, only one that would earn him another curl of that lovely, carmine lip. Besides wasn't it true that an old man could do his job, couldn't Jack?

But there was another argument. Perry was well aware of his father's failing health, well aware that he'd relinquished direction of the mill, well aware of the extra strain that would be placed on him, if he left. Shouldn't he bite the bullet, accept the slurs, the accusations of cowardice for his father's sake? Wasn't it his duty to soldier on on the home front? Nathanial was in uniform. Wasn't that enough? No, he knew of families in Over Darren with four sons serving. But in the end all his reasoning faltered before the fact that a beautiful girl had called him a coward.

That night after dinner he produced the white feather. They were in the family dining room, in the round room, sitting at a round table. The room was well lit by two tall windows and French windows to the terraced garden.

Doreen had just cleared the table and left the coffee. Esther had always wanted a butler, but Jack wouldn't hear of it.

"I'm not having a tailor's dummy standing there, watching my every mouthful."

Esther had not been able to budge him on this. They'd had Doreen since she was a little girl. Now she was a plump, homely body. Jack it was who consulted her about meals.

"A nice bit of brisket with all the works tonight, Doreen."

"Right you are Jack."

Esther's dream of butler, housekeeper and a retinue of servants came true only once a year when they had their annual Christmas at-home for Over Darren's high society, an event heartily detested by Jack.

There were just the four of them. Jack, Esther, Perry and Evelyn. Jack had a mug, all the others had fine china.

"A young woman gave me this," Perry explained.

"Whatever for?" Esther demanded.

"I'm sure she'd like to volunteer for King and country!" Evelyn declared.

Jack waited, watching his son, who was twiddling the feather back and forth.

"Now lad, you're not going to take any notice of a daft lass."

"It's not nice being thought a coward."

"Who thinks that?" Esther demanded.

"Nobody's going to say that about Nathanial," Perry went on.

"You don't think he's going to volunteer for the front do you?" Jack said. He'll make sure he's on Hoddersdale's staff, well out of harm's way."

"He might not have a choice, if this war lasts any length of time." Perry said. "Anyway the point is he's in uniform and nobody's going to call him a coward."

"Perry, I tell you frankly, I'm not a young man anymore. This war's going to bring a lot of work in. I'm not sure I'm up to it."

"What are you talking about Jack?" Esther demanded. "There's nothing wrong with you. I'm the one who's ailing."

"Why don't you let me help?" Evelyn said.

Everyone ignored her.

"I just asked a question. Why can't I help?"

"You know nothing at all about the business," Jack said.

"I can learn."

"It really isn't that simple, Eve," Perry said. "I've worked my way up."

Evelyn snorted.

"A week in every department and then Father makes you a director."

"I'd like to see you do it."

"I will."

"You wouldn't last two minutes."

"Just let me try."

Jack was irritated by this distraction and tried to quash it.

"Work in weaving for a week," he said, "and I'll give it some consideration."

"Right I will." Her face was flushed.

"Evelyn, think what you're saying." Esther said. "How can you work with all those common people?"

"When can I start?"

"Six in the morning," Jack said. "Come into the garden Perry. I want to say something."

It was her eyes that gave it away. Rose's eyes were dark and flashing like her daughter Sadie's, but there was no other resemblance. Rose's eyes were deep-set, in a face wrinkled by the passing years. Rose's lips were twisted awry by her stroke, her body crippled, her hair dull and grey. But those eyes lit up, when she saw Ben on the doorstep. She did a little mime to try and convey the message that Sadie was out, but would soon be back. She ushered him inside, showed him to a chair.

Like many houses in Over Darren this one had just the two rooms: one downstairs, one up, with a scullery at the top of the cellar stairs. There was no back door. It was a back-to-back. There were rows of houses like this, rows and rows, ranks and ranks, drawn up on the town's hills like an army.

The room was poorly and sparsely furnished, but it was scrupulously clean. Brightly coloured rag rugs covered some of the stone flags. There was a statue of St Anthony of Padua on the sideboard and a crucifix on the wall above. Touches which gave the room an exotic air to Protestant Ben.

They sat in silence.

Ben had been put out to find Sadie not at home. He'd been hoping to bring up his grievance piping hot and compel her to accompany him for a walk. He'd no quarrel with Rose, knew she thought well of him and approved of him as a suitor.

Rose's hearing must have detected her daughter's approaching step. She gestured towards the door

Sadie stepped in from the street, flushed and glowing, as though touched with glory by the setting sun. She was not pleased to see Ben. She hid her annoyance by turning and hanging up her hat behind the door. She'd been for a rendez-vous with Nathanial, and he had not turned up. She wanted to be alone to deal with the turmoil in her heart.

Rose indicated that she would leave them to talk.

The only other room was the solitary bedroom, but she bustled off there, as though heading for the west wing.

"I saw you with him," Ben hissed.

Sadie's colour heightened.

"Who?"

"Don't pretend, Mick Moon. Who else?"

Anybody else would have seen Sadie's relief, seen she'd been let off the hook, but not Ben. He was too agitated.

"We were just walking in the park."

"You never walk in the park with me."

"Oh Ben."

"I suppose it's because I'm not in uniform."

Sadie's plight swept all before it. She'd no time for anything else. As she contemplated it, she even forgot Ben was there.

"Is it?" he insisted. "Would it make any difference, if I was in uniform?"

"Oh Ben."

"Would it? Say the word and I'll go and enlist. Just say it."

Sadie just wanted him to go, and didn't really care where to. She needed to think, to be by herself, to consider her options. She just wanted Ben out of the way. He complicated things.

"Do you?" he insisted, and he trembled, and was flushed, and there were even tears starting to his eyes. Sadie despised him at that moment. What were his problems compared to hers? What did he know about love and passion and broken hearts?

"Yes," she said, "Join up. That's the best thing you can do, for both our sakes."

"You know I will do," he said, more quietly.

"Good, go and do it then."

Ben slammed out of the house. Sadie turned her face to the ceiling and closed her eyes, and then she heard her mother coming down the stairs. She groaned and hugged herself and felt sick to her stomach.

Chapter Eight

Evelyn felt self-conscious walking through the streets of Over Darren in the early morning among the crowds of men and women making their way to Empire Mill. She was wearing old, unfashionable clothes, but still stood out like a butterfly among moths. Her snug, well-cut jacket and her smart, neat boots couldn't be more different from the drab uniform of shawl and fustian, clogs and calico of the army of workers.

Gatekeeper Joe Glover's equanimity was threatened. He was renowned for being unmovable when late-comers begged to be let in. No excuse would work, not illness, nor accident, nor bereavement. He would sit, brawny arms folded, in his gatekeeper's booth and shake his bulldog head.

"If it was Lord Kitchener stood there, if it were King George himself, he wouldn't get in."

Being confronted by Jack Shaw's daughter, saying she was starting in the weaving threw him.

"I've had no instructions, Miss."

"That's all right. I'll wait in the office, but make sure you tell my father I was on time."

Joe nodded and watched her slim form cross the mill yard.

"There's going to be some fun and games," he said to himself.

Jack's temper was not improved when he learned Evelyn was there.

"I'd hoped you'd have thought better of your mad idea."

"It wasn't an idle whim, Father. I meant what I said."

"Eve, it's not a nice place to be," Perry pleaded.

"Other women do it."

"They're brought up to it," Jack said. "They have a hard life from the minute they're born."

"Mother was a weaver," Evelyn pointed out.

The reminder that his delicate, ailing wife had once survived in such an environment gave Jack pause.

"It will make things difficult for the other workers," Perry said.

"I don't expect any special treatment."

"And you'll get none. Come on lass," Jack said and led the way towards the roar of the weaving shed.

Evelyn's misgivings began as they neared the source of the noise. Jack had a word with the weaving manager Frank Pearson, resting his hand on his shoulder and shouting in his ear. The man gave her a quick look of astonishment, opened the weaving shed door and was seemingly sucked into the maelstrom within.

On Evelyn's face was an expression Jack hadn't seen since she was a scared little girl on her first day at school. His heart went out to her. He had to shout to explain that he'd sent for Becky who was going to train her.

Becky Flynn was a flame-haired woman in her forties. She was Sadie's aunt, having married Rose's brother. She was not overawed by Jack. She looked Evelyn up and down and did not seem impressed.

"Look after her, Becky," Jack yelled.

Becky nodded and taking Evelyn by the arm led her into the weaving shed.

The noise was a palpable thing and made Evelyn stagger. Her thoughts fled before its onslaught. She had to force her way forward. It was like entering an alien and totally hostile environment. And yet all around her folk toiled, tended and inspected cloth, seemingly oblivious to the din. She was appalled. Had it not been for Becky's firm grip, she would have fled.

"Who've you set on to train her?" Perry asked.

"Becky," Jack said.

Perry gave a low whistle.

"Red Becky, is that wise?"

"Do you think they'll fight?"

"Either that or become fast friends and then we *have* got a problem."

After the doctor had examined his teeth, heart, chest and eyesight, after he'd taken the New Testament and sworn to serve His Majesty the King, his heirs and successors and the generals and officers set over him, Ben was in the army and was at once aware of a slight adjustment in the manner of the recruiting Sergeant. The leather-faced, gravel-voiced old sweat's veneer of civility was gone. The sheep's clothing had been removed and the big bad wolf stood in front of him, red in tooth and claw.

"You're in the army now lad, and here's your first week's pay."

As he pocketed the silver, Ben felt he'd made a pact with the Devil. The Sergeant seemed to have no more to say. Ben hesitated then asked.

"Where do I go for my uniform?"

"Uniform! Do you think Kitchener has nothing to think about but your blooming uniform? You'll be asking for a rifle next."

Ben was at a loss. The Sergeant enjoyed his discomfiture for a few minutes before adding:

"I know what it is, you're itching to get over there and drive Jerry out of France, but first things first. You just turn up on the Mill Field in the morning and we'll start by forming fours. Right get a move on. Here's another likely lad wanting to fight for King and country. How old are you lad?"

"Seventeen, sir," the lad replied, his girlish complexion colouring.

" Sorry lad, these ears are playing tricks. It's all them years in the artillery. You did say eighteen, didn't you?"

"Yes sir eighteen sir, sorry sir."

"That's the spirit. Now just go and see the doctor over there and we'll get you sworn in. And here's another hero ready for the front."

By now there was a queue and Ben left.

His momentous decision now seemed of no moment. Had he expected to walk out of the recruiting office the epitome of soldierly manhood? No, but he'd expected something to change. He was now a private in the Lancashire Territorials, but he felt the same. He looked the same. No change was in prospect.

Sally-Anne's response was low key. Only the rapidity of her rocking back and forth in her chair betrayed her.

"I suppose it had to happen. I'd have felt ashamed if the other mothers had sent their sons and you'd been still at home, but it's a bad business."

Old Barker, chief clerk at Empire Mill shook his hand.

"We'll miss you my boy, but you're doing your duty and there'll always be a job here for you when you return."

Sam had stared at him in frank astonishment.

"After what they did to us! After being beaten for walking on God's own land, on our birth-right. After seeing the brutal face of our ruling class, you're going to fight for them! What argument have you got with the ordinary German worker?"

"Come now Wainwright. Let's have less of that kind of talk," said Barker, the wing tips of his celluloid collar all a quiver. "Young Preston's only doing what's right. You might well take a leaf out of his book and fight for King and country."

"Not me. I'll not fight their wars for them. Oh it's my country when they want me to lay down my life, but it's not when I want a walk in the hills."

"That's more than enough Wainwright. Get on with your work."

Becky was 45, single, opinionated, argumentative, fiery, outspoken, free-thinking. She was tough and wiry, bony-faced, with a flame of red hair and emerald eyes. She could have made herself attractive, but disdained to do so. She was always ready to help her fellow women at Empire Mill, and was as likely to find herself at loggerheads with the union, as the managers.

Evelyn was too preoccupied trying to cope with the weaving shed environment, with trying to understand what Becky wanted her to do, to be able to arrive at an opinion of her trainer. Becky though had chance to study her pupil.

It was only at tea-breaks that the two women could communicate properly, and even then Evelyn's ears were ringing. Although she didn't know it, Evelyn's chances of sticking it out for a week depended entirely on Becky. If she got her on her side, then the other women would support her, if not then they knew how to make it impossible for her.

"What do you want to spend a week here for?" Becky asked outright, when the two of them were sitting on a wall in the mill yard. Evelyn, sipping from a cracked mug, which was all Becky could find for her, knew that suggesting she mind her own business wouldn't advance her cause, and felt she was too much out of her depth, too overwhelmed by the noise, by the demands of the machines to put on airs, or to attempt to put herself in a good light, so she told the truth.

"My father's worried about the future. My brother Nathanial is already in the army and he's afraid Perry will follow. He doesn't think he can cope with them both gone."

"That doesn't sound like Jack to me. Is he not well?"

"Not really, but he won't see a doctor."

"Too frightened to find out what's wrong. That's men for you.

But how does you working here help?"

"I said I'd take Perry's place, but they just laughed; 'what do you know about business?' My father said if I could stick a week in the weaving shed, he'd take more notice of my idea."

Becky liked the idea of a woman in management at Empire Mill. She liked Evelyn's pluck and enthusiasm too.

"There's so much needs doing to help the people who work here," Evelyn went on.

"Jack's not a bad employer," Becky said, "not as bad as some."

"Yes, but look at what some do; building garden villages for their workers, providing holidays."

"Can't see a garden village being built here, and even if it was, there's still the smoke and grime and folk breathing in cotton fibres."

Evelyn thought of the pure air on Cara.

"Come on lass." Becky said. "Let's get back to it. Don't you worry we'll get you through the week and you'll be well on the way to being a bonnie weaver by the end of it."

Chapter Nine

The Reverend Charles Pomfret made the most of the war. He thundered at the Germans from the pulpit of St Jude's on Sundays. He exhorted, nay commanded the men of his flock to enlist. When the Derby scheme came in, encouraging men to register for military service, he volunteered to administer it and was assiduous in his duties, collaborating with the town's librarian Ephraim Neville to compile a list of men of military age.

The two of them launched a scheme to solicit donations of books and magazines to send to the troops and Mr Neville took upon himself the melancholy task of compiling a roll of honour, culling details of casualties from the Over Darren Gazette. Both men became special constables. Both men involved themselves in home defence.

They were not the only prominent professional men in the town doing their utmost for the war, their utmost in every respect but one – that of volunteering for service overseas themselves.

Reverend Pomfret's visits to Woodlands were much pleasanter with Evelyn absent at the mill. He had Esther to himself and could exert his charm and insinuate his suggestions with no worries that sharp eyes and sharp ears were observing him, taking note.

He talked a good deal about his recruiting efforts, about brave men and proud mothers, about Christian duty and God's will. He left her in no doubt that Satan led the German host and God led our own boys. He praised Nathanial and sighed over Perry's civilian status. He induced Esther to think that Perry really should go, that the war would soon be over and Jack could manage in the interim.

It suited his still unacknowledged scheme, a scheme forming in his mind, but which he dare not examine, which he dare not admit to even to himself. It suited him to have Nathanial and Perry out of the way. He was unmovable in his conviction that whatever he had to do to gain his object was permissible, was morally correct, was indeed approved of by God. Was he not God's representative? Was he not to all intents and purposes God?

When they'd spoken in the garden Jack had confessed to Perry that he feared for his health, that he didn't know how much longer he had.

"See Dr Howard, Father, for goodness sake," Perry had said.

"I've never seen a doctor in my life and I don't mean to start now."

It had been on Perry's lips to say 'Let me have a word with him for you,' but he knew his father would veto that, so had kept quiet.

"What's the matter anyway? What are the symptoms?"

Jack had described the shortness of breath, the chest pains, the feeling of being detached. 'I'm just getting old, lad.'

Later Perry had visited Dr Howard at his villa residence in East Park Road.

"Sounds like heart problems, but I need to see him."

Dr Howard was an irascible Irishman, not much loved but respected for his skills.

"If it is, can you do anything?" Perry asked.

"Yes, there are medications to thin the blood and lower the risk of heart attacks."

"Leave it to me. I might not get him here, but I'll try and get him to see you at Woodlands."

"I know Jack Shaw. He's a tough old bird. There's no reason he can't live another twenty years."

Ben's debut as a private of the Lancashire Territorials lacked martial pomp. In his work suit and straw boater, he was standing with fifty similarly dressed men on the Mill Field being addressed by Captain John Forrester, of Forresters Chartered Surveyors and Auctioneers, a long established Over Darren business. It had been Captain Forrester who had done so much under Lord Hoddersdale's guidance towards raising the Lancashire Battalion. He was well known by builders far and near for his zeal and attention to minute detail.

Ben knew most of the men around him. They were neighbours and old school fellows, or from Empire Mill. Indeed in his own section were two from his form at the Board School: Dougie and Nobby. Standing next to him was a man he knew just as well: Smithy. He was older than Ben, but a good head shorter and with a stoop that projected his head forward somewhat. He had a sour expression on his thin suspicious face and had all the makings of a promising barrack room lawyer.

Captain Forrester explained that they were going to learn how to form fours, turn left, turn right and about turn.

"I notice he's got his uniform," Smithy muttered out of the side of his mouth. Forrester was indeed splendidly turned out. His uniform was of the finest cloth and cut and his Sam Browne belt gleamed like a mirror. Ben did not reply. He was preoccupied with dismay at the sight of the drill Sergeant Major, former mill foreman Happy Frank, who had answered the call for former NCOs to return to the colours.

Making the most of his inches, Happy Frank stood ramrod stiff.

"Quick march!" he bawled.

The company lurched forward.

"About turn!"

Some turned. Some stopped. Some went straight on. A shambles resulted.

"Knock them into shape Sergeant Major," Captain Forrester ordered and left the field.

"Leave it to me sir." Happy Frank saluted smartly.

"I've never seen such a shower of Mary Anns," he bawled walking up and down and prodding men into line with his stick.

By now there was quite an audience round the perimeter of the field, men and women from the mill in their break and idlers from the town.

"It's like being in a blooming circus," Smithy complained.

"What's that?" Happy Frank demanded. He approached, but as soon as he recognised Ben, he forgot all about Smithy's interruption.

"It's you is it? I'm going to have my work cut out with you. At ease! Not you Preston. Six steps forward Preston. Let's have a good look at you."

Ben wished he'd never gone near the recruiting office. Hoping for admiration and status, he was being made an object of scorn. Happy Frank pulled off his straw boater and skimmed it away. Lifting his hair with his stick, he bawled

"You need a visit to the barber's. Don't come on the parade ground in this state again. Attention!"

With some hesitation Ben assumed an erect stance.

Frank pushed his face as close as he could to Ben's

"Is that the best you can do?"

"No, sir."

"Well why didn't you do your best?"

"Don't know, sir."

Frank cocked an ear

"What's the matter, lost your voice? Shout it laddie, shout it!"

"Don't know, sir," he bleated.

It was Ben's worst nightmare: to be the object of everyone's attention. Already he could hear laughter.

"You don't know! Well if you don't I'm sure I don't. Quick march, Preston. Come on. Lift them feet up, higher, higher. Left turn. Quick march, left, right, left, right."

Sergeant Frank ran alongside him.

"Is that the best you can do, Preston? Right turn! Right, not left. Don't you know your left from your right?"

The crowd rippled with laughter. Ben was glowing. His wits scattered by shame and confusion. It was some time before he noticed a figure had emerged from the crowd and was approaching unsteadily, and further moments passed before he realised that it was his father.

"Right Private Preston, let's see what you're like at running on the spot. Come on you Mary Ann, what are you staring at?"

His father tapped the Sergeant on the shoulder.

"Oy chum."

Sergeant Frank wheeled round. He was about to order the intruder off the parade ground, when a looping blow hit him on the side of the face and sent him sprawling.

The men behind cheered. The crowd applauded. Ben urged his father to make himself scarce.

"You haven't a couple of bob on you son?"

Ben fumbled in his pocket and gave him his army pay. The glow of it lit up Jimmy's face. He gave a stage wink, a thumbs up and veered off, listing badly. The crowd greeted him with cheers and back slapping.

Sergeant Frank was still hors de combat. The company began to disintegrate, men drifting away.

"Come on," Smithy urged. "Best not be around when that little rat comes to his senses."

And that was the last time the battalion drilled in public. The assembly room in the Town Hall became the preferred venue

Chapter Ten

The German plan had failed. With the help of Britain's 'contemptible little army', the French had halted the German advance. The quick victory that Germany had hoped for, before it turned to deal with Russia, had not been achieved. Now it would have to fight on two fronts. On the Western front it dug in on the high ground. It constructed formidable defences, trenches with timber and concrete lined bunkers, communication trenches, reserve trenches, all dug deep, all rooted solidly in Belgian and French soil. Dense entanglements of barbed wire were created, many feet high, many yards deep, an impenetrable undergrowth with barbs of finest German steel, which protected the German front line. Thousands of machine guns were dug in at vantage points where they could sweep no-man's land and clear it of anything that tried to move. Thousands of guns were brought up and deployed in batteries:

howitzers, field guns, heavy guns. Millions of men, well trained, well equipped, hard, highly motivated troops were in place all along the front line and in reserve. Poison gas was stock piled. Flame throwers were being developed. The Germans had no intention of going anywhere.

The British Expeditionary Force, a professional army of seasoned troops had been able to stop the German advance, but it was too small. There was not enough artillery. There was not enough ammunition, but most of all there were not enough men. The British Army needed men, hundreds of men, thousands of men, millions of men. And in drill halls, parade grounds and camps all over England men were being trained and equipped, and in foundries and factories up and down the land guns were being made and shells were pouring off assembly lines. Hundreds of thousands of horses were being bought and shipped off to France. Although lorries, buses and even taxis were at the front, horses were needed to cope with the terrain and the mud.

For the individual soldier who had enlisted, full of patriotic ardour and keen to spill German blood, it seemed they'd never get to France. Many feared it would all be over before they got their chance. August went by, September went by, October went by November went by. Christmas was coming and still they were training, still they were square bashing, still going on route marches, still doing bayonet practice. Rumours abounded – they were off to France; they were off to Egypt, and indeed some were shipped off, but for most, the training went on. The wait seemed interminable.

After his public humiliation Ben kept away from Sadie. He felt acutely how ridiculous his position was: rushing to enlist to copy his dashing rival, he'd only made himself a laughing stock. If he'd only remained aloof, if he'd disdained to enlist, his position would have been better. He did the training every morning. He listened to the lectures in the afternoon. He stayed at home and read the paper in the evening. Some of the others Smithy, Dougie and Pat would meet for a drink, but not being a drinking man, Ben stayed away.

He told himself when the uniforms came he would go and see

Sadie, but when they did come, because of the shortage of Khaki, they were blue serge.

"We look like blooming postmen," Smithy complained. And indeed they did, so Ben stayed away.

It took years to make a good weaver, but Evelyn was a quick learner. She was nimble fingered and intelligent and once she'd got used to the appalling noise, she made good progress. She learned to tie weavers' knots. She learned the knack of starting the loom with the shuttle pushed well back in the box, so it got the full force of the picking stick. She learned to stop the loom with the warp threads in line, and most crucial of all, she became adept at catching the weft before it broke or ran out. There were weavers who worked all their lives and could never get the knack of that and the pieces they wove were spoilt as a result.

Neither Evelyn, nor Becky were typical of their class and background. Both had ideas which startled their peers, but although both were prepared to dismiss preconceptions and see others as fellow human beings, the constraints upon them were at first too great. Becky was well aware that Evelyn had all the power on her side, how ever much she downplayed it, and Evelyn knew she mustn't undermine her father's position by being too frank.

When she got her pay packet though Evelyn could not conceal her shock.

"Is this it for working all week?"

"You're just a learner," Becky pointed out.

"Well what do you get?"

"A few bob more."

"Is that all?"

Evelyn was not an extravagant woman. She kept well within the allowance her father made her, but what Becky earned was a negligible sum, what she might spend on a hat, or a visit to a Manchester theatre.

"It's not right," she said staring at the paltry amount in her hand, a hand that after only a week was crisscrossed with little cuts from the weft and nicked by contact with machinery. "It's not right that we should have so much and you so little."

Becky had to say what she felt.

"No, it's not right, but it's the way things are."

"I should talk to Father."

Becky reached out and held her arm.

"It's not that simple. Even if he listened, what could he do? He already pays better than some. If he paid more he'd have to put his prices up, and he'd lose customers. No it's not Jack Shaw's fault. He just took his chance. I dare say he works hard enough. It's the system that's wrong, the capitalist system."

Becky thought she'd said enough.

She could have gone on, could have let off some steam, could have pointed out that while some folk can afford islands with fine homes on them; others couldn't afford to put a bit of supper on the table. She could have pointed out that the wealth of the idle rich came from the sweat and aching muscles of the poor, that the factory system was little more than slavery, but she said nothing, because, all other considerations aside, she felt sure she would soon be approaching Jack Shaw asking for help.

"You go tell your father you've the makings of a good weaver. I'll tell him so myself when I see him."

Evelyn pushed her wage towards Becky.

"Take it please; you've been a tremendous help."

Becky had to restrain herself. She could cheerfully have thrown it in the young woman's face. She could easily have said; 'keep it. It'll be the only honest money you'll ever earn in your life,' instead she said.

"Put it in the plate on Sunday. I'm sure Reverend Pomfret will put it to good use."

Lord Hoddersdale had got his battalion. He'd got his 1,000 men. The Lancashire Pals would soon be on the move at last. When word of it first came through, it was treated as a false rumour like all the others, but on a drear December morning Captain Forrester made the announcement: the men would march to the station the following day and thence to camp.

"Bloody marvellous, isn't it?" Smithy said, "soon as winter arrives, they send us camping."

Faced with not seeing Sadie again for who knew how long, and maybe never seeing her again, Ben overcame his humiliation and his postman's uniform and sought her out on the market. Her stall was empty. He asked the women gossiping at the next stall. They exchanged looks.

"She's not well, love," one said.

"She's at home," said the other.

Ben hurried away. The women exchanged looks again and plunged into excited speculation.

Their reaction stoked Ben's morbid imagination. The reaction of Rose on the doorstep did nothing to allay his fears. She left him there, and he heard an exchange of fierce whispers. At last she let him in.

Sadie was by the fire with a shawl over her knees. She didn't look well. Her high colour was gone. There were shadows beneath her eyes. Her manner was fluttery and febrile. Her voice seemed to come from far away.

"What is it? What's the matter?" Ben asked, his young face flushed with concern.

"Oh it's nothing. I'll soon be back to normal."

"But, what is it?" Ben insisted.

"Women's troubles."

Ben flushed an even deeper scarlet. Sadie watched the colour come and go on the delicate skin of his face.

"We're leaving. We're off to camp tomorrow. I thought I'd come and say goodbye."

"I'm glad you did. You take good care of yourself."

Ben couldn't keep some of his bitterness from bubbling up.

"I suppose you've been seeing Mick Moon."

She shook her head.

"No, he's in France."

The knowledge brought him no relief. While he'd been playing at soldiers in his postman outfit, Mick had been doing the real thing.

"Sadie when I get back… if I get back…when it's all over…"

"Don't Ben. Let's just leave it. Let's just see…"

"Will I see you again?"

"Definitely, something tells me that. Something tells me you'll be alright." She held out her hand. He took it and squeezed it. It felt hot; Sadie's hand. He couldn't see her properly for tears. He couldn't speak. He left.

The next morning was grey and cheerless. The sun was a distant, pale disc smothered by layers of grey. A piper in kilt and bonnet led the men from the drill hall to the station and there was a crowd to cheer them, family, friends, neighbours and workmates. Sally-Ann was not among them. They'd said their goodbye after breakfast, inarticulate, emotion-choked goodbyes. They were not able to express affection, never hugged. In the early years of her marriage, Sally-Anne had poured out her woes and bitterness to the infant Ben, who while not understanding had withdrawn inside himself to escape her misery.

There was a good deal of singing and horseplay on the train, but Ben didn't take part. All he could think of was that every moment was taking him further away from Sadie, further away from home, with no guarantee that he was ever coming back.

Chapter Eleven

At Christmas at Over Darren, the Theatre Royal was showing the latest images from the front and, it was claimed, the 'greatest war picture ever produced' - 'Within the Enemy Lines.' There were numerous concerts for the Mayor's fund and the Belgian refugees were entertained at the assembly rooms in the Town Hall. Young carol singers added 'La Marseillaise' to their repertoires on the doorsteps in honour of our glorious ally.

Most shops put on their Christmas displays as usual. There were no shortages: Valencienne raisins; Tunis dates and Napoli walnuts were all available, but at higher prices. For those sending Christmas gifts to the front, Hargreaves' tobacconist offered pipes of all kinds, boxes of cigars and packets of tobacco. Gents outfitters Laceys had khaki worsted socks, pure wool underwear, woollen helmets, mufflers and gloves.

German cruisers had shelled Scarborough and Whitby causing many casualties and damaging the old abbey. There were many in Over Darren who had been to the resorts in the wakes week and were shocked that where they had sauntered in shirt sleeves had come under enemy fire.

Reverend Pomfret published a sermon in the Gazette reminding readers that Christmas was a Christian celebration, not a pagan orgy of feasting and self-indulgence, a time to reflect upon Christian duty, which, for the young men of the town who had not already done so, meant enlisting to fight God's foe.

The Gazette also noted the Christmas post arrangements: three deliveries per day as usual up to Christmas Day, when there would only be one and when the Post Office would close at noon. In France postal services were being built up to make sure mail got to the men. Even front line troops could expect letters from home to arrive within a few days. The Army knew how important it was for men's morale to receive regular post.

In France and Flanders the fields were white with snow. In Over Darren it was unseasonably mild, damp and misty.

Jack Shaw liked Christmas. He liked to have his family round him, liked to have good food, good fires, liked to be generous with presents. What he didn't like was the Christmas 'at home', which had become a favourite with Esther. The Mayor came along with sundry aldermen and councillors. The Town Clerk and other town hall bigwigs came. Jack's great rival Sam Birtwistle of Lister Mills came, as did other smaller fry from the town's commercial life. Any number of clergy came, headed of course by Reverend Pomfret.

Esther adored the occasion. Planning for it occupied most of December. It was her big opportunity, her chance to twinkle in society's firmament. Jack resented every penny spent, begrudged how it eclipsed Christmas, begrudged how it took over Woodlands, until he felt a stranger in his own home. Extra staff had to be hired of course; Doreen couldn't be expected to cope. Indeed she resented it as much as Jack, resented having her kitchen invaded. For days florists and caterers were coming and going.

An incongruous addition to all the hustle and bustle approached one morning. In her shawl and clogs Becky Flynn was trudging up Perseverence Lane to Woodlands. Carts and motor lorries bearing provisions for the occasion passed her by. There was a long drive that wound round by tall rhododendrons. The carriers all made for the rear of the house. Becky went up to the mausoleum-like front entrance.

Much to Esther's chagrin Jack would answer the door himself if he was around. She thought it beneath the dignity of the family to do so and expected Doreen to trail up from the kitchen. One of the maids hired for the occasion answered Becky's ring.

"I'm here to have a word with Jack."

The girl was nonplussed. Becky had an air of authority, but her accent and dress belied it. Becky resolved the difficulty by pushing past her into the hall.

"Just go and tell him Becky Flynn is here. He'll see me."

The maid had stepped back, but was still unsure. Esther happened to be in the hall supervising the dressing of the Christmas tree, 'a present from Lord Hoddersdale', she was fond of saying, conveying the impression that his lordship had scoured his plantation for the perfect specimen himself, when in fact he knew nothing about it, the tree having been given to Nathanial by the Estate Manager, currying favour with his lordship's future son-in-law.

"You're looking well Esther lass," Becky said," but by God you've put on some weight."

She was well aware of Esther's humble beginnings and wasn't about to let her put on any airs. Esther sent the maid away to fetch Jack before Becky could embarrass her any further. Becky admired the tree.

"It's a grand'un."

"It's a present from…" Esther thought better of saying where it was from. "It's a present."

"And very nice too, but I don't think I could fit one branch of it in our parlour."

Jack appeared.

"What's to do, lass?"

"Can I have a word, Jack, in private?"

Despite the impending occasion, Jack was in a good mood. He'd agreed for Dr Howard to come and had been reassured as a result.

"You're in good shape Jack Shaw," Dr Howard had said, "but we just need to keep an eye on your heart. No doubt your father had the same trouble."

"Aye he died of heart failure."

"Well there are pills I can give you. Take one a day, but keep them handy, and if you have an attack, breathlessness, chest pains, pains in your arms, take one right away. With luck you've another twenty years ahead of you."

Jack lead the way to his study where there was a good fire. He stood before it, warming his backside, waiting for Becky to speak.

"There's no easy way to put this Jack, so I won't try. My niece Sadie's expecting and your lad is the father."

Jack had been expecting some complaint about Evelyn, not this.

"Perry!"

Becky brushed the notion aside.

"Nathanial."

"Nathanial, but he's engaged to Lord Hoddersdale's lass!"

Becky said nothing, but her expression was eloquent.

"Are you sure?"

"Ask anybody on the market. Nathanial's been hanging round her stall like a wasp round a jam pot."

Jack recovered himself and set his face, expecting some hard bargaining.

"You want me to make him marry her?"

"I do not. Do you think she'd have him? No I want some provision for the lass and for the bairn that's to come. Sadie's Rose can't do a lot, crippled as she is."

"You can't prove it's Nathan's."

"Well lad, we can have a good try. There's plenty of folk'll swear they've seen them together in that fancy motor of his, and it's not as if their paths would cross much in the normal course of things." She didn't elaborate, knowing it would be more effective to let Jack work out the consequences for himself.

Jack was certain Becky was telling the truth. He knew what a fool Nathan was, but he was his son for all that and he'd no desire to see him dragged into a scandal.

Becky watched the thoughts follow one another across the old man's face.

"It'll be your grandchild," she said softly.

The thought had already occurred to him: Sadie's child would be his grandchild, legitimate or not. And what did that matter? It'd still be Shaw blood in him.

"Sit down Becky. Will you have a drink? There's whisky and sherry."

"A drop of whisky'll keep the cold out when I'm walking back."

"You don't need to walk. Dickens will drive you back."

Becky knew when someone was trying to soft soap her. She perched on the edge of the chair and sipped her whisky, no less determined to have what's right.

Jack sat too, leaning forward, his elbows on his knees. She looked at him and shuddered, and it was not the whisky going down. There was something in the old man's face. There was a shadow there. She could see the cataracts forming in his eyes, the broken veins that empurpled his nose, his well-weathered cheeks, his white hair, white moustache, the slight tremor in his thin purple lips, but there'd been a flash of something else, an intimation of mortality.

"You're not well, Jack."

He waved the notion away with his glass.

"What's she like this Sadie?"

"She's a bonnie lass. I'm not surprised your lad fell for her. But there's more to her than that. She's a hard worker. She runs that stall on her own. She'll be a good mother."

"Well this might be the only grandchild I'll ever get to see, so this is what I'll do for her; I'll send her to Cara, to the big house. She can have the bairn there, and she can keep the place decent for when we go in the spring There'll be no scandal, no gossip."

"That suits you, of course,"

"Aye it does, but her too."

"What's it like this Cara?"

"I never knew there was such a place. If there's a heaven on earth, it's there. That'll be the place for me when I've finished here."

"You can't expect the lass to keep a big house decent on her own."

"There's her mother."

"She can't do so much. What about me going, just to make sure the place is fit?"

"Do you think I'm made of money?"

"I know you are. Anyway you're getting three servants for nothing more than their fare and keep."

"You strike a hard bargain, Becky Flynn, but then I remember your father Ike could talk the birds out of the trees. We'll call it settled. Go and see Dicky Pearson in the wages office." He changed the subject. "How did Evelyn go on?"

"Oh she's right enough that one. I've never had a quicker learner. She could be a big help to you running the mill."

"She told you that did she? Anyway she's been in the office these last few weeks and Perry's said much the same."

"Well why don't you give her her head, see what she can do?"

"Maybe I will."

Before Becky left, she warned.

"If Sadie doesn't like the place, we'll be back."

"She'll like it and so will you."

Becky's news had shaken Jack. It had caught him unprepared and although he felt pleased at the way he'd handled it, he was reminded of how unpredictable things were, of how the ground could shift under your feet. His heart went out to Sadie's unborn child. He knew full well if Nathan had children with Hoddersdale's daughter, he wouldn't get a look in. They'd be brought up at the nursery at Hoddersdale Hall in a manner that would create a gulf he would never be able to bridge. He was determined to make Nathan see he had an obligation there and wondered if he should change his will to make proper provision for the child.

He had to dress for the dinner, another thing he loathed. Perry helped him with his tie. There was something in the lad's manner that jarred, something false about his joviality. Jack took his place at the dinner table, feeling ungrounded, detached. The glittering silverware, the candles, the snowy linen, the brilliant chatter, the steaming dishes swirled around him, all slightly blurred.

They came back into focus very sharply, very painfully, when he was aware that the Reverend Pomfret had stood up to speak.

"Ladies and gentlemen, may I just have your attention for a moment? It gives me great pleasure to introduce an old friend of all of us in a new guise. Please welcome 2nd Lieutenant Peregrine Shaw of the Lancashire Territorial Regiment."

There was much applause, 'here heres', 'bravos', and tapping on glasses.

"Take a bow, Perry," Reverend Pomfret said, applauding vigorously himself. He bent his head to Esther, " A proud moment for you dear lady," he whispered.

It was indeed. She was in raptures. Over Darren's society round her table applauding her son. Nathan reached over to shake his brother's and brother officer's hand. Perry accepted the congratulations, but avoided his father's angry look. Evelyn came up behind him, squeezed his shoulders and whispered.

"Don't worry Daddy. We'll manage things between us."

He patted her hand, but said nothing.

As soon as he could do so without causing comment, Jack went to his study. There was something he had to do. He took pen and paper and wrote an addition to his will to the effect that Sadie O' Donnell, her mother and child to come have the right to live at Achaglass House until the child reached the age of 21 and that £200 per year be settled on the child from his estate. He knew his signature would have to be witnessed, but wanted to get it recorded.

Prompted by some predatory instinct, by a sense of a tryst with destiny approaching, Pomfret had noted Jack leaving and had followed him. He tapped on the study door and walked in.

Jack glared at him.

"I suppose you encouraged this nonsense of Perry enlisting."

"It was his mother's wish."

The reverend gentleman was normally the last person Jack wanted to see, but realised he could be useful.

"I'm signing this addition to my will. Be good enough to witness it for me."

He handed it over and the Reverend Pomfret began to peruse it.

"It's no business of yours man. Just sign."

"My dear sir. I can hardly sign something the import of which I have not studied."

"It's my will. Just sign it."

"I don't understand. Why should you settle money on the brat of an Irish tinker? The workhouse is good enough for them."

"Just sign it will you?"

Pomfret was wondering how he could make use of this knowledge. In his frustration Jack rose and threatened to move round the table.

"Very well, as you wish," Pomfret said and bent to add his signature.

Something gave in Jack's chest. The room lurched and began to dim.

"The pills!" he gasped. "There on the mantelpiece."

"Where, which pills?" Pomfret's own breathing became laboured as he realised a moment of crisis had arrived, a moment that could advance his schemes.

"There the white box…"

"This one?"

"Yes, quickly…quickly man…"

Pomfret toyed with the box and watched Jack, who was leaning heavily on the desk and reaching out. What should he do? If he delayed and Jack survived, how would he explain his delay? Then Jack collapsed on the floor and he'd been at enough death beds to know by the old man's colour that it was unlikely he'd ever be called upon to explain.

He waited still though, waited till all signs of life were extinct, until Jack's glare was fixed meaninglessly at the ceiling, waited still longer, then with the pills rattling in his hand spilled the box by Jack, pocketed Jack's addition to his will, then hastened to sound the alarm.

Chapter Twelve

Ben and his section spent the days before Christmas guarding the main line of the Great Western Railway. They were still in their blue serge and were armed with staves. 'Camp' was Carstairs Hall, a forlorn and long-deserted country house in a mournful valley. They slept on floorboards in gaunt, high-ceilinged rooms amid the debris of plaster and laths.

Ben's overriding emotion was homesickness. He'd never been so far from home. His heart ached as he thought of his old routines, his old haunts; the damp streets, the gas lamps, the corner shops, the sound of his mother getting the ashes out of the range, all the trivial things he'd taken for granted for so long, that were now gone, and might never come back.

Contrary to orders Smithy abandoned his station and walked along the line to Ben.

"What's the blooming point of this? What are we supposed to be guarding it against?"

Smithy's unremitting gloom chimed on the whole with his own mood. He got on well with the men in his section: 'Liverpool Pat,' 'Dougie', the ex-tram driver, gormless Nobby, even 'Yorky', an overbearing former slaughterhouse man from Leeds. Their NCO Sergeant Sutton was an old sweat who'd seen service in South Africa and was as relaxed as a man in his position could be. He had the features of a non too successful boxer, a thin moustache and there was usually a sardonic grin on his face.

And in counter point to the dull ache of homesickness, was the sharp pang when his thoughts came round again to Sadie. Was she any better? Did she think of him at all? He pictured her moving among familiar scenes, all unaware that she was now far from Over Darren, with much further to go.

Although mild for December, the dampness made it chilly. It was dark, the darkest day of the year. The year was at its lowest ebb. Ben's new boots were tight. He stamped his feet to keep the circulation going. He knew it would be a long bruising battle of attrition between his feet and the leather before they achieved a comfortable co-existence.

The zealous Captain Forrester had set them the task of guarding the railway. When he left to dine with fellow officers, Sergeant Sutton ambled along the line and stood the men down.

It was colder in the old hall than it had been outside. Many years of chill had accumulated. They lit a fire of lathes in the massive hearth space and stood around it with outstretched hands.

"Blooming crackers making us guard a railway line," Smithy grumbled.

"Look well if it's missing in the morning," Pat joked.

They eased their belts and took off their packs. One or two pulled off their boots.

"Hey Nobby go and scrounge some wood," Dougie urged.

Nobby set off, but then bethought himself.

"You go!" he squeaked indignantly.

"Come on lads," Pat said. "We'll all go. We'll need a fair pile to see us through the night."

The first thing a soldier learns are the arts of foraging and scrounging. They came back with buckets of coal, armfuls of logs and Smithy had snaffled some potatoes from the cook's store.

They sat or squatted around the fire poking potatoes into the embers. Their shadows did red Indian dances on the walls behind them. Later Sergeant Sutton came round and smoked a pipe with them.

"What's it like Sarge, going over the top?" Dougie asked, his honest face reddening, aware of his own innocence.

"You'll find out soon enough."

"What if you can't do it?" Pat asked, laughing at the notion. "What if you freeze?"

"Then an officer comes along and puts a bullet through your head."

"Blooming marvellous isn't it?" Smithy said. "You can go and get shot by the enemy, or stay and get shot by your own side."

"What's to be scared of?" Yorky demanded. "You've got your bayonet. Fritz can't stand up to a bayonet charge. I've spent my life working with cold steel. I know how to cut a body open. Have his liver out in no time."

"What's a Yorkshireman doing in a Lancashire regiment?" Pat asked.

"They send us over to give you lot a bit of backbone."

"I tell you something, my muscles have tightened up since we came here," Nobby announced. It was his speciality, sprinkling conversations with irrelevancies. Everybody knew to ignore him.

"Weren't you scared the first time you went into action, Sarge?" Dougie asked.

Sergeant Sutton took the pipe out of his mouth.

"Everybody's scared lad, first time, second time, every time. Only a fool wouldn't be scared, but you'll be alright. You'll do what has to be done, and you'll do it because of your pals. The Army's not daft. Why do you think it recruits men from the same town, the same factory, the same street and puts them all together? Because it knows you won't let your pals down. It knows you don't want your pals going back and saying so and so's funked it. You'll be alright because you're not fighting for King and Country, you're fighting for your pals. Right I'm off. Don't be up half the night gossiping. We're moving on tomorrow."

"Where too Sarge?" they chorused.

"You'll find out soon enough."

The battalion moved to Bedford, to a real camp, under canvas, and of course the weather turned much colder, much to Smithy's morose satisfaction. They took the place of the Loyal North Lancs who had gone to France. Here they got their khaki uniforms at last and began to learn the intricacies of webbing and puttees. They got their rifles, short magazine Lee Enfields and learned how to dismantle them and put them back together. Here began their serious training: digging trenches and filling them in again, route marches, bayonet practice, shooting practice on the rifle range.

The rifle felt oddly familiar to Ben, as though he'd been reunited with a missing limb. He'd fired air rifles at the fair to win misshapen pot dogs for Sally-Anne, and the rifle seemed like an old friend. He seemed to have a memory of firing it long ago. He found he could fire accurately and rapidly, but above the crackle of musketry and the shouts of the NCOs, he thought he heard other sounds, the thunder of big guns, the chatter of machine guns, the cries of men. And when the spent cartridges were flying past him and the whiff of cordite was in his nostrils, he felt a rising distress, a sense of panic. On one such occasion, he got up on his knees and loosed off a whole clip of ammunition in less than a minute, tearing the distant target in half

"Here Sarge, have you seen Ben's shooting. Fritz doesn't stand a chance," Dougie said.

"Nice shooting Private Preston," Sergeant Sutton said quietly, but as he observed Ben's agitation: his pale, drawn features, the tremor in his hands, he thought to himself, 'this lad will either get a VC, or be shot for cowardice.'

"Watch where you're pointing that thing!" Smithy yelled as Nobbie, intent on examining his jammed mechanism was pointing the rifle this way and that.

"He should have that taken off him," Yorky said.

"It's not my fault there's something wrong with it," Nobby squawked.

"There's summat wrong with you," Smithy grumbled.

They went on route marches, eighteen, twenty miles with full packs weighing 60 pounds dragging on their shoulders. Bedford was bitterly cold. Its hedgerows were white and a freezing wind moaned over the white fields. Ben's feet took a good pounding. Every night his socks were stiff with blood.

They slept under canvas and were cold all the time. The night skies were clear and teemed with blazing stars. They learned to keep their boots under the blankets, otherwise in the morning the leather would be frozen stiff and they wouldn't be able to get them on.

On Christmas Day the men were well fed, and Bedford Amateur Thespians put on an entertainment. They all had thoughts of home. Ben pictured Christmas dinner. Sally-Anne would make it. Cuthbert, his sister Maria, her husband Herbert and the little ones, Philip and David would come round. No doubt Jimmy would turn up on the doorstep at some point and there'd be a row. Herbert though would seize this excuse to escape and escort him to the Stag's Head.

It was freezing hard at Ypres in France. The Germans had Christmas trees in their trenches and placed candles and Chinese lanterns on the parapets. Thinking it was a signal for an imminent attack, the British opened fire. All that came over were the sounds of the Germans singing carols: 'Heilige nacht, stille nacht'. The British ceased fire. Orders were that there was to be no fraternising, but when unarmed Germans appeared in no man's land, the braver souls climbed out to meet them. Some of the Germans had worked in England and spoke good English. They exchanged cigarettes and the Germans, who were Saxons, rolled a barrel of beer over.

Officers met and agreed a truce. English and Germans worked together to bury the dead and stood heads bowed while the Lord's prayer was recited. They showed each other photos of their loved ones. They swapped addresses. There was a football match. The Germans won 3- 2. The truce lasted until midnight on Boxing day and then they started shooting each other again.

It was at Bedford camp that they learned of Jack Shaw's death. Many of the men had worked for him or known him. He'd been a major figure in Over Darren for decades past. He'd towered over the landscape as much as Empire Mill chimney. The landscape would not be the same. Over Darren would no longer be the same place.

Ben remembered when he was a boy and Jack Shaw used to call on his Granddad Cuthbert. The two men would sit and smoke and yarn about characters they had known, about the hard days when folk struggled to put food on the table, when parents had to see their children go hungry. They would relate tales their fathers had told about the loom breakers and the riots of the 1820s, about Peterloo and the suffering of the workhouse children put to work as slaves in the early mills. Before he left Jack would always find a copper or two for Ben to spend at the sweet shop.

To think of Over Darren without Jack made it seem even more remote, even less attainable. Impossible now to go back to how things had been.

Chapter Thirteen

Jack's death did change the landscape. Over Darren no longer was the same place. Empire Mill did seem diminished. Even the towering campanile seemed less imposing.

In her extravagant grief Esther had wanted Jack buried in the grounds of Woodlands and a mausoleum built, but she was persuaded at last that he would want to be in the old cemetery at Whitehall with his parents and sister Alice.

The Reverend Pomfret would have welcomed him at St Jude's, but had to settle for conducting the funeral ceremony. He eulogised Jack. He made him a paragon of all the virtues. He smothered his memory with flowery phrases, coated it with sugary sentiments, until nobody there recognised him. They shifted uncomfortably in their pews, and old Cuthbert standing at the back muttered:

"Why couldn't he just say: 'he could be a right awkward bugger, but all-in-all he were a decent chap, and we shall miss him.'"

Esther had to be supported by her sons at the graveside. It was a bright day. Raucous rooks mocked the ceremony. The mourners stretched from the grave all the way through the hillside cemetery to the gates, a black column that spread out around the grave, where there was a splash of colour where the flowers had been laid.

Flags in the town were at half-mast. Many folk wore black arm bands. Empire Mill was closed. In many streets curtains were drawn, but many would have been drawn anyway to mark other bereavements. Letters were already arriving regretting to inform the recipients of the death of their sons or husbands.

There were no more bright days that January. The days that followed were shrouded in freezing mist. Time seemed to slow down. It was as if Jack had been a vital component and the year could not get on without him. The brief, pale days were buttressed by black, ice-bound nights and would not budge. January went on for ever.

Nathanial requested an interview with his future father-in-law and Brigadier, Lord Hoddersdale. It took place in his lordship's office, which overlooked the frozen ornamental lake.

"I was saddened to hear of your father's death." Hoddersdale spoke with great formality and no warmth.

"Yes sir, thank you sir. That's what I wanted to see you about. My brother Peregrine is a 2nd lieutenant in the battalion now. We need to put father's affairs in order."

"There's no one else to run the business?"

"Only my sister and mother, sir."

"So it will have to be sold."

"That seems the likeliest course, sir."

"Very well, you'd best talk to Captain Forrester about this, but the battalion does not move to France for some considerable time yet. As you will have discovered, it takes the best part of a year to turn a raw recruit into an effective soldier. I'm sure you'll be granted time to put your father's affairs in good order, but I expect you both in camp by the end of the month. I shall be arriving myself soon after to make an inspection."

"Yes sir. Thank you sir."

Nathanial didn't know whether to salute or not. He hesitated, looking at Hoddersdale for a clue, nothing was forthcoming, so he repeated his thanks and left, feeling acutely what a minefield to negotiate it is, when your prospective father-in-law is also your Brigadier and a peer of the realm.

There were no surprises in Jack's will. Incomes were provided for Perry, Nathan and Evelyn out of the estate, otherwise everything went to Esther: Woodlands, Empire Mill, the isle of Cara, everything was unconditionally hers.

Reverend Pomfret learned the details with great satisfaction. He'd been afraid there might be conditions, the one he'd feared most was that Esther would forfeit all if she remarried.

St Jude's was a relatively new church built to serve the thousands who flocked to work at Empire Mill. It was on the town's upper slopes. Pomfret's home, Ashleigh, was further away still, by a path that was a popular route to the moors. Resenting incursions on his privacy, Pomfret had had the path closed, barring access to ramblers and others. He'd gone so far as to bring actions for trespass against persistent offenders, Joe Wainwright being one of them.

Pomfret brooded in his study at night, allowing his plans to take shape. It was as though he were a necromancer calling up familiars, or images of the future. Maybe he feared that anyone passing by might see, might see into his heart, might see the terrifying scope of his ambitions, might see the ruthlessness of his pursuit of them. Sure that he was doing God's will, there was nothing he wouldn't do to achieve his ends. The only person who saw, the only person who watched was his housekeeper Jane Holden, but so negligible was her presence that Pomfret was never aware of it.

Night after night he considered the codicil to Jack's will. What could it mean? The obvious conclusion to draw was that the child the trollop was carrying was his own. Why else would he provide for it? He'd not heard the gossip about Sadie and Nathanial. He was too remote from the ordinary folk of Over Darren to be privy to that kind of tittle-tattle. Knowing what he did of Jack though, he found it hard to think of him as a philanderer. He knew Sadie, knew such dark, gypsy good-looks could only come from the Devil. Whether it was true or not that Jack had strayed, couldn't he use the doubt it cast on his fidelity to further his cause? Couldn't he use it to undermine Esther's foolish worship of his memory?

Becky and her family travelled north, unaware of Jack's death. To Sadie Scotland seemed as remote as Newfoundland and in that lay its appeal. She wanted to be as far away from Over Darren's condemning gaze and gossip as possible. She'd protested at first at accepting favours from Nathan's family, but Becky would have none of that.

"You've to swallow your pride Sadie O'Donnell. Think of the child. They owe you this much, if not more. Besides I don't think Jack Shaw was displeased at the prospect. He might do more for his grandchild yet, if he lives long enough."

"What do you mean, if he lives long enough?"

"I felt his time was near, and that he knew it too, or a part of him knew it."

"So if he turns up his toes, we have to come back."

"That doesn't follow. Jack's no fool. He expects us to make ourselves useful. He's got himself three staff for nothing more than our keep. Daft as she is, I dare say Esther would keep us on the same terms."

Sadie sat in the corner of the compartment in the train going north, enveloped in her cloak and enveloped in her cares. The cheeky attentions of a couple of soldiers could not get through to her, nor the polite apologies of the young officer who sent them packing.

The metropolitan magnificence of Glasgow did not touch her, nor the grand scenery of Lochs and Bens that succeeded it. Only when they were on the steamer, only when she was looking at the western isles with the sun going down beyond, did she become aware of her surroundings.

She stayed wrapped in her cloak by the ship's rail, and her face glowed again with something of its old beauty. She'd only ever seen the sea at Blackpool, where it struggles to get itself noticed with all the seafront attractions, the Tower and the densely packed beach.

Here was a new world, a world undreamt of by someone who'd grown up surrounded by grimy streets full of smoke-blackened buildings, where even on the brightest days the sun's rays were filtered through smoke. Here was clear water. Here was blue sea, green sea, cobalt sea, golden sea. Here were tremendous skies, rose-tinted skies, skies shot through with purple. Here were magic isles with granite cliffs, white beaches and far off peaks.

She looked and her dark eyes filled with tears that rolled unchecked down her face.

They landed late and by the time they reached Achaglass House it was dark. They could make nothing of it, just a black shadow against the deep blue, star-strewn sky. Tam, the garrulous shop-keeper from the village, who had the keys showed them in and made valiant attempts to draw them into conversation, but Becky shooed him away and the three of them were left alone in the vast, dark, silent house.

Chapter Fourteen

The route marches continued. The digging and filling in of trenches continued. The bayonet practice, the rifle practice continued. The bitter cold continued. The cold was ever present. They were cold during the night. They were cold when they turned out in the morning. They were cold all day long. Only in moments of exertion, digging and marching was there any respite.

The 51st Highland Division arrived one night and camped next to the Lancashires. In the morning when Ben went to fetch water, some of them were nearby, big, tough-looking men in kilts speaking in an incomprehensible dialect. Ben stared. One of them, a long-faced, long-limbed fellow turned and managed to make himself understood loud and clear.

"What's up wi'you, you English bastard? Have you no seen a real soldier before?"

Ben flushed with dismay.

"Sorry."

"Sorry are you? No as sorry as you will be."

"Look at his face, Robbie," his comrade urged. "He's blushing like a lassie."

"Well it's normally against my principles to strike a lassie, but I'll make an exception now."

"What's up?" Yorky demanded, coming to see what was delaying his shaving water. He put some beef between Ben and his would-be assailant.

"I'm just going to teach the wee lassie some manners."

"Oh aye, and what would you know about manners, haggis head?"

The Highlanders stirred, squaring up to Yorky. By now Pat, Smithy and the others had appeared.

"Punch him in the face Yorky," Smithy advised. "It can only improve it."

More Highlanders and more Lancashires were arriving, but among them were Sergeant Sutton and a Scots NCO.

"Right lads back to your ablutions," Sergeant Sutton ordered.

The Highlanders stood their ground, but confronted with the chunk of Highland granite that was their own sergeant, they reluctantly dispersed.

Whenever their paths crossed, Robbie continued to torment Ben, taunting him, mimicking him, making obscene gestures. It became a matter of concern, a matter of honour to his section members.

"Blooming marvellous, isn't it?" Smithy observed. "Fritz is supposed to be the enemy and we end up fighting the Jocks."

"You're going to have to give him a blooming good hiding," Dougie said.

"Tell you what," Yorky said. "Tell him you'll see him on the shooting range for a scrap. We'll be there and give him the beating of his life."

"He'll bring his pals with him," Smithy said. "You can bet your life."

"So much the better," Yorky said. "We'll give them a good

thumping an'all."

Ben was grateful for the advice, but was fairly sure he wasn't going to follow it, but a seed must have been planted, because unsuspected by all, least of all himself, a bloody climax was coming.

They met in the boardroom at Empire Mill: Peregrine, Nathanial, Evelyn, Eddie Moy, the company solicitor, Old Hindle, and the company accountant, Cyril Ellison. Esther had refused to attend, refused to admit that life had to go on, that something had to be decided about the future.

Nathan was quite certain they should sell.

"There are difficult times coming. You and I will be overseas Perry. Empire Mill can't run itself. Who's going to make the decisions?"

"I am," said Evelyn quietly.

"Oh Eve!" Nathan wailed. "You don't know the first thing"

"No, you're wrong," Perry said. "She's picked up quite a lot in the last couple of months."

"But not enough to run the biggest weaving concern in Over Darren," Nathan said.

"A lot depends on what Mr Moy thinks," Evelyn said. "You're right of course Nathan. I couldn't do it single-handedly, but I can learn and I can listen to advice, and if Mr Moy can work on that basis, then I'm happy to take the responsibility."

Eddie Moy, bald, middle-aged and irascible, made more so by a chronic ulcer, ran his finger round the inside of his collar. Jack's criticisms had sometimes made him explode and walk out, but he had always thought better of it and come back and apologised. He knew the business thoroughly, having worked up from being a weaver. He was hard-headed and shrewd, safe but cautious. 'Steady as she goes' was his motto. He saw his future as more certain with Evelyn at the helm, than if the business was put up for sale. Besides he was sure the war would be over by Christmas and Perry and Nathan would soon be back.

"I think we could manage, but I tell you frankly I'd expect an increase in salary. However you look at it, I'd have a lot more on my plate."

"I wouldn't object to that," Evelyn said.

Perry turned to Old Hindle. The lawyer was a survivor from the Victorian era. He still had the high wing collar and pince-nez. It was said of him that he rarely smiled and if he did it boded ill for somebody. But despite his curmudgeonly manner, he was meticulous, efficient, far-seeing and loyal to the Shaw family. He didn't approve of Evelyn at the head of Empire Mill. He didn't approve of women in business at all, but since the war had begun women were doing all kinds of jobs traditionally reserved for men, but he too expected Nathan and Perry would soon be back and it would be business as usual.

"It's not a good time to sell, as I'm sure Ellison will agree."

"Hindle's right." Cyril said. "We're losing workers to the munitions industry. They can pay higher wages than we can. Furthermore if the war goes on much longer and the Germans continue their attacks on our shipping, cotton is going to be in short supply. They're not going to fill ships with cotton when we need food and ammunition. I fear the Government may ration supplies. My view is we'd be better to go on as we are with Miss Evelyn at the helm and review the situation in a year's time."

Perry paused to see if anybody had anything to add. Nobody did.

"Well I'm inclined to accept what's just been said. Have you decided objections to Evelyn being Chairman, Nathan?"

Nathan was quite sure his future father-in-law would not approve, but he had neither the interest nor the energy to oppose it. He shrugged.

"Have it your own way, but I don't see any good coming of it."

So it was formally minuted that Evelyn be appointed Chairman and Eddie's salary be raised. Evelyn experienced a thrill of triumph, not unmixed with apprehension.

Back at Woodlands Perry and Nathan packed and were driven to the station to catch the train south en route for camp.

Soldiers were kept hard at it. There were not many minutes in the day when they were not drilling, marching, digging, cleaning equipment. The Army knew it was not wise to let the men have too much time for reflection. Those not on guard duty, or doubling up and down the parade ground as punishment for some transgression, usually had an hour in the evening when they could write home, read or play cards. It was in that hour when things finally came to a head between Ben and Robbie.

The Highlanders had wandered over to Ben's section, at leisure outside their tent. As soon as he saw the anticipation of fun on Robbie's face, Ben felt the blood throb at his temples and his vision swam.

"Hey lassie, are you no writing to your man?"

Ben's face reddened. Robbie hooted.

"Look at that, she's as red as a turkey cock."

Ben's face was red, but it was not a flush of embarrassment, it was a flush of blinding anger.

Yorky, who had been painstakingly putting together a letter to his wife, retracted his protruding tongue, which had purple marks on from his indelible pencil, and prepared to settle the Highlander's hash, but Ben rushed past him.

The fury of Ben's attack took Robbie by surprise and he was unable to fend off the flurry of blows. He was forced backwards, but he rallied, counter-attacked, and got some short, solid punches into Ben's head.

At the foot of the trench ladder, in the half-light of dawn Ben waited. Whistles blew far and near. There were shouts and some ragged cheering. He began to climb but the man behind him held him back by his webbing.

"Wait, not yet, let the gunfire pass."

Machine guns rattled and red tracers arced across the pre-dawn sky. Bullets kicked over the mud and debris at the rear of the trench. Men were already falling.

"Now, now, quickly!"

Ben took the strain of his many burdens, bombs, trenching tools, wire-cutters, ammunition and hauled himself out of the trench, climbed out into no man's land. He went forward at a crouch. The advancing line of men ahead had already thinned. The light was sickly yet, not strong enough to banish uncertainty. The German front line was a black profile against the dawning day, spitting red tracers which flew like hornets. Whenever a bullet struck home, he could hear it and the involuntary gasp or cry the man made before sinking into the ground.

Avoiding shell holes was a preoccupation. There were fewer men to follow now. Some seemed to be veering away, off course. Then the shelling began, shells began screaming overhead, each with its own demonic song, each holding its own hellish note until the ground-shaking detonation. And the ground would barely have stilled, before another shook it and another and another. A frenzy seized the world, a storm of whirling bodies and parts of bodies, mixed up with mud, debris, smoke, fire and steam from the water-filled craters.

In the eye of the storm Ben lost all notion of which way was forward, which way was back. He stumbled along as the world disintegrated around him. Dawn had fled and night had returned. Only the flash of explosions showed him the shell holes brimming with multi-coloured water, the tangle of bloody barbed wire; and the restless dead being endlessly turned, tormented and torn asunder by mad giants, enraged that their toy soldiers would no longer stand up.

Chapter Fifteen

The prevailing Scottish weather had reasserted itself on Cara - wind and rain. The skies were variously grey and the rain fell. Sometimes it came down hard, sometimes it came down gently, sometimes it came down almost imperceptibly, but it rarely relented. Sometimes the wind ran out of cloud to weave and there was an interlude of cold blue sky and cold sunshine.

They'd spent an uncomfortable first night on the chairs by the kitchen range, not wanting to venture into the interior of the many chambered house. It had seemed a vast labyrinth into which they might disappear, never to return.

In the morning the fire had all but gone out. Sadie mended it, while Rose fetched water and Becky went down to the village for provisions.

Cara was ten miles long and five miles at its widest point. There was one road that ran the length of it, and a rough road it was, becoming nothing more than a track at either end. The village by the harbour was the only settlement, otherwise there were only isolated farms. The high land was in the west, Ben Blea the only hill at barely 300 feet. The pine forest started beyond the garden wall of Achaglass and stretched to Ben Blea's upper slopes. There were many white beaches, notably Carraig Na Mor on the western shore.

Becky wrapped her shawl around her against the driving rain. It was Christmas Day, but no sign of any celebrations. Fishing boats were going out. Smoke flapped from chimneys of the long, low cottages. Gulls clamoured. Cattle lowed and pails clanged from within byres where milking was in progress. The island was famous for its cheese.

The shop was low and dark and cluttered with sacks and bins, jars and tins of all shapes and sizes. Tam was the shopkeeper, doubling as postmaster, booking clerk for the steamers and agent for Achaglass. He had bushy eyebrows, protuberant features and a bony frame. His eyes were his most remarkable feature, wild, staring and all seeing.

"You're making yourself comfortable?"

"We're managing."

"I couldn't help seeing the lassie, will it be your daughter, is carrying a child? I expect her man's at the front."

Becky didn't deny it.

"Aye well my own boy Robbie is there with the Argyll and Sutherlands. There's only we old folk left on the island now. Even the girls have gone to the munitions in Glasgow."

Esther ordered eggs, bread, flour, milk, sugar, cheese, bacon, dried fruit. As he ducked and dived gathering it all together, he fired his questions.

"Is he a good man to work for, the new Laird?"

"Middling."

"Is that so? We thought very well of him. Is that Minister that was with him family?"

"He would be, if he got the chance."

"Is that how it is? We didn't take to him, no we didn't take to him."

Becky found the old man's curiosity amusing and was determined to give little away. A woman came into the shop. Her broad face glistening with rain. Her grey locks were plastered to her forehead.

"Good day to you Mary," Tam said. "This is Becky, one of the Laird's people. They're up at the big house, putting it straight for the new Laird."

The woman's pale-blue eyes widened.

"Up at Achaglass is it? Och that's a cold, dree place. And it's no just the damp. There's something aglay about it."

"Och Mary, don't talk such nonsense. All it needs are fires and people to live in it. And there'll be a bairn born up there soon. Becky's daughter's near her time."

"She's my niece," Becky corrected and was at once vexed for falling into his trap.

"Och your niece is it, then the lady with the wry face and the limp'll be the lassie's mother."

Becky didn't deny it. Mary's delight at the coming birth was evident on her honest face.

"The wee laddie'll be a real Islander."

"It might be a lassie," Becky said

"No, no it'll be a laddie."

"You'll have to forgive her, Becky. She has the sight, as they say in the Isles."

"It's the Celtic blood," Mary said. "You'll have it yourself Becky, with red hair like that. Now if you need ought at all for the bairn - crib, blankets, come to my cottage. It's the first one past the harbour wall."

Becky realised their curiosity was well merited and not malicious.

"Come up to the house tonight and we'll have a Christmas drink," she said.

"Och we don't keep Christmas," Tam said, but the prospect of gleaning further information was too much. "It'd no be neighbourly though to say no."

They breakfasted on toast and eggs and strong tea and then

explored the house. The meanness of the servants' hall contrasted with the opulence elsewhere. No expence had been spared in the latter, none gone to in the former. The maids' bedrooms were narrow cells with a deal table in the corner for a water basin and jug. They chose one each however and Rose stripped off the bed linen for washing.

Bare walls in the servants quarters, but in most of the rest of the house there was panelling of golden oak, with ornate plasterwork on the ceilings. They counted the bedrooms - eleven of them on two floors, most with heavily curtained four poster beds, handsome fireplaces and adjoining dressing rooms with smaller fireplaces.

Rose hefted a coal skuttle and pantomimed having to trudge along with it.

"And bring up water in the morning," Sadie said.

"And light all the fires downstairs," Becky said.

Fires were just what the house needed. It smelled of damp. Even without the rain, moist sea breezes were rarely absent. It needed a good clean too. The windows were grimy. Dust furred every surface.

There was a library, a billiard room, morning room, day room, two reception rooms, and the great hall. Most of the rooms had tall windows commanding sea views, views which were grey and foreshortened on such a damp day.

"Well we've plenty to do," Becky said. "Jack, the old devil, has got a good bargain. Never mind we'll not break our backs today of all days. We'll make the kitchen right and start on the rest tomorrow."

Rose cleaned the range and black-leaded it. Sadie tackled the knives, forks and spoons. Becky baked a cake and took stock. There were tinned and dried foods, rice and lentils in the pantry. There were home-bottled preserves and honey in the kitchen cupboards. The door to the cellar was next to the larder. She took a lamp and ventured down. Wine bins stretched as far as she could see. What lay beyond was lost in shifting shadows. She didn't think Jack would begrudge them a bottle or two on Christmas Day, so took two dusty, cobwebby bottles back up with her.

"Tam and the rest of them will be coming to pick holes," Becky said. "Let's make sure they're disappointed."

They polished copper and brass till it gleamed. They scrubbed tables till they were white. They swept and sanded floors. They washed down walls and made windows sparkle. Becky went out beyond the garden into the forest, and came back with a small fir tree. She set it in a bucket, placed it in the window, fixed tapers to the branches and lit them. They banked up the fire. There wasn't a cosier, cheerier kitchen on the island.

At Sadie's urging they wrapped up warmly and went out to look at the sea. It was running high and white crests raced like tiny yachts in the narrows between Cara and the grey profile of the mainland.

The wind whipped Sadie's dark hair in and out of her eyes. It had brought a healthy tone to her cheeks. She clutched the cloak at her throat and shivered, but her dark eyes gleamed.

"I like it here," she shouted, her voice carried away by the wind. "It feels like home."

"Not much like our home," Becky said.

"That's not home. This is."

So far north in winter, it was soon dark. Their guests arrived with lamps.

"Good evening to you ladies", said Tam. "This is my good wife Meg."

Her frame was along the same bony lines as her husband, but it was her inquisitive manner and bright, searching eyes that made her seem more like Tam's twin than his wife. She surveyed the kitchen.

"My you have been busy." She surveyed Sadie. "Och you've forgotten to put your ring back on dear."

"Yes I'll look for it later." A smile, that was part embarrassed and part mischievous, dimpled her face .

"We've brought you some oatcakes," Tam said. "They'll keep a good while in the tin."

The heads of the pair of them were twisting this way and that, and their eyes swivelling hither and thither, so anxious were they not to miss a thing.

Muffled up, Mary came in, followed by a tall, well-weathered, well-whiskered fisherman.

"This is Gus, my man," Mary said. "We've brought you a herring, fresh out of the sea this morning."

Gus handed it over with a solemn wink.

"You've made yourselves at home in the kitchen." Mary said. "I don't mind it in here, but I wouldn't put a foot in the rest of the house for all the herring between here and the Devil's Point."

"It's just the damp," Tam insisted. "I mind when Colonel Scarlet had it built my father saying 'it's ower big and too near the sea. They'll never keep the damp out.'"

"There's more than damp got in," Mary said darkly. Tam tutted.

Rose put out the cake and Becky offered them drinks.

"I've just brought this up from the cellar. I don't know what it's like."

"The Laird's wine, Tam declared and his eyes sparkled in anticipation. He held his glass aloft. "Och it's clear as a bell. It'll be fine. Shall we drink to the laddies overseas?" He addressed Rose. "I dare say your man's at the front too.".

Rose mimed her lack of speech and Becky explained that her husband had been killed many years ago in a pit explosion.

Tam and his wife regarded Rose with wide eyes, frankly fascinated by her condition.

"Och and I bet there was no compensation at all," Tam ventured.

Rose shook her head. Tam's gaze swivelled to Becky, who forestalled him.

"I've never come across a man that was my equal, and I'm not going to marry beneath me."

Two pairs of bushy eyebrows shot up.

"Well here's to our Robbie," Tam said, when he'd recovered his composure. "And what's your man called dear?" he asked of Sadie.

Sadie blushed deeply, then raised her glass.

"Ben. He's called Ben."

The wine lubricated the conversation and the evening passed pleasantly enough. Becky enjoyed parrying the prying questions.

Mary cast uneasy glances at the door to the house. Gus said not a word. They didn't stay late. The rain had stopped and there was a moon to light them home.

When they'd gone, the three women opened the second bottle and lingered by the fire.

"When you toasted Ben just now," Becky said. "Were you just putting the bloodhounds off the scent, or did you mean it?"

Sadie stared at the glowing coals.

"Oh I don't know. He's just always been there, too much so. I've taken him for granted I suppose."

Rose wagged a finger at her.

"Oh I know you think I should have encouraged him, but where would we be, if I had done? In a one up one down in the shadow of Empire Mill."

"Better than being Nathanial Shaw's cast-off," Becky said.

"Oh I don't mean I wanted what he could have given me, I mean this place, the island. You can see things here, see the things that matter."

"Imagine if some of the poor folk in Over Darren, coughing the cotton dust out of their lungs could see this place," Becky said. "They'd think they'd died and gone to heaven."

"Let's have a last look at the sea," Sadie urged.

"We'll all catch our deaths," Becky complained, but she took up her shawl from the back of the rocking chair and wrapped herself up in it.

The sky was clear, but for a few tiny clouds, whose silver linings gleamed through. The sea had calmed and there was a silver causeway across it to the mainland, now a black profile.

AchaglassHouse was black too, but for the window where the Christmas tree glowed. Above the roof were suspended countless shimmering stars.

The baby stirred within Sadie, as though it too were moved by the beauty and wonder of it all.

Sadie felt at peace with herself at last.

Chapter Sixteen

Esther had turned Jack into a saint. She'd lost all idea of the man he'd been. In the morning-room, in the room where she passed her days reclining on a chaise, she had created a shrine. There were not many photos of him, but she'd found one from the year he was President of the Cotton Manufacturers' Association, taken at the annual dinner, when he was trussed up in formal evening attire and looking thoroughly uncomfortable. In front of it she'd placed his pipe and his gold pocket watch, which had stopped. She'd turned the hands back to the time of his death. There were flowers round the photo, and each day she discarded them and arranged fresh ones. She spoke to him.

"Jack dear, how are you today? I've not slept well, hardly a wink. It's not the same on your own. I'm tossing and turning all night. One minute I'm too hot, the next I'm too cold. I don't know what'll become of me. I won't be long behind you, Jack. I can feel it. I won't make old bones."

It angered Doreen to hear her going on so. She resented the way the real Jack was being lost.

"He'll say summat back to her one of these days, and that'll settle her hash."

The Reverend Pomfret found it disconcerting too, but for quite different reasons. Now that Jack was gone, Nathanial and Perry away with the Lancashires at camp and Evelyn often at the mill, he had as much access to Esther as he could wish for. In the early weeks after Jack's death, he'd encouraged her to think his soul lingered lovingly nearby, unable to part from her. He indulged her delusions about Jack's perfections, seeking to become indispensable to her. But then the difficulty arose. How was he to press his cause as a worthy successor to Jack, when she'd elevated him so, deified him almost? How many times did she declare:

"He was the most wonderful man who ever lived, the most perfect husband. We never had a cross word."

She would reach out and clasp Pomfret's hand and, with tears in her eyes, declare:

"There's not a man alive to be mentioned in the same breath. I was so lucky to find him. There can never be another, never."

Many's the night he sat in his study at the vicarage, as dark and brooding as the moor above. What would the consequences be, if he showed her the codicil to Jack's will; that Jack would be swiftly dashed from his pedestal and she would turn to him for consolation? But there were two difficulties. What would she make of the document? It could be said to have legal validity. He'd no desire to hand the Irish tinkers the right to live on Cara for the next 21 years. He'd other plans for Cara. But then it was hardly likely that Esther would insist on Jack's wishes being carried out, hardly likely that she'd want to see right done by his bastard child and paramour. Much more likely that she'd want the tinkers cast out of Cara for good and all.

But the second difficulty was how to account for having the will in his possession and for the fact that his signature was on it. His story had been that Jack had asked to see him after dinner and that he'd arrived at the study to find him lying dead, with the pills scattered everywhere. He knew Esther's intellect was not the sharpest. He'd not have relished close questioning by Perry or Evelyn. Surely he could be confident that she'd be so overwhelmed by the revelation that she'd take flight to some absurd extreme and never question the detail. But suppose she did.

He would have to admit to having abstracted the will. He would say he did so from the noblest motives; to protect her from scandal. The will was dated of course, so he'd have to say he'd witnessed it under protest earlier that day, but when he'd found Jack later, the will was still there on his desk. He would say he was sure Jack had summoned him to say he'd had second thoughts, and that by concealing the will, he was only carrying out Jack's wishes.

Pomfret was wily enough to know there were contradictions, loose ends, trip wires everywhere, but he relished such challenges. He was carrying out God's will and the good Lord would see him through. Only let Esther agree to marry him and let the will be destroyed, and he'd be safe enough. He would do it. He would show her the will and trust to his wits and persuasive powers to see him through.

One bitter March morning, he went to his bureau and opened the secret drawer that contained the will. It was not there. Baffled, he stepped back and stared round the room. He remembered putting it there. He remembered thinking it was safe enough there. He'd looked at it not three weeks ago. He remembered sitting in the gathering gloom, with the will on his knee, hatching his plans. Had he not put it back? Had he put it somewhere else? He searched through his other papers, his correspondence, his share certificates, deeds, Doctor of Divinity papers, the letters from his mother. He flung open cupboards and dragged out drawers, until the disturbance brought Jane to his study.

"Is everything alright, sir?"

He glared at her. Could she...? No, her every fibre wilted with passivity. What would such a document mean to her? She wouldn't have the wit to seize its implications. Her apparent meekness and docility enraged him. Her very existence was a reproach to him. That she should call him 'sir', when it was her money that had secured Ashleigh stung him.

"It's nothing. It's nothing. Get about your business."

"Will you be in for lunch, sir?"

He wasn't going to let this stop him. If by some wild chance he'd underestimated Jane and she thought she could obstruct him, then she was very much mistaken.

"No, I will not. I will dine at Woodlands with Mrs. Shaw."

Jane bowed her head and dwindled away.

Pomfret stormed out. He would not be beaten. If anything this set-back had fired him up. The prize was all the more worth winning now. He had his carriage brought round and rattled away down the frosty lane to Woodlands.

Chapter Seventeen

Evelyn really only needed to be at the mill for the monthly board meeting, but to Eddie Moy's annoyance, she appeared most days, conscientiously studying the books and asking questions about everything he did. Unlike Jack she didn't go round the mill finding fault, but although Jack's criticisms had irked him, he'd known Jack was usually right. Evelyn was always wrong, just wrong, so fundamentally wrong that he didn't know where to start to put her right.

"The wages are far too low," she said.

"Try telling that to them as work for Billy Birtwistle, Miss. They'd give an arm and a leg to be working here."

"Are you saying we can't improve the operatives' conditions?"

"You've done enough by carrying on the business. If you'd sold out, like as not Billy Birtwistle would have bought us up, and we'd all have been on less, those of us that still had a job that is."

The truth was Jack Shaw had been a good employer. Although a mill owner now, his forbears had been workers and Jack had not forgotten his grandfather's tales of beatings and cruel treatment. He was not without sympathy for the workers.

"What about doing something for their welfare?" Evelyn insisted

"That's for the unions to worry about," Eddie said, "and they push us hard enough, believe me. We're here to produce high quality goods and make a profit, nowt wrong with that."

"But some heads of business build model villages for their workers. Surely if the operatives knew we had their welfare at heart, they'd work harder, more conscientiously and there'd be no need for all these rules and regulations."

"Don't you believe it, Miss. I know them. They'd take any relaxation of discipline as a sign of weakness and we'd be out of business in a month."

Evelyn had walked over to the window to look down at the mill yard.

"What about an annual outing paid for by the firm?" she asked, struck by sudden inspiration.

Eddie passed his hand over his face. He could feel his ulcer twingeing. 'No wonder Jack died of heart attack,' he thought, 'if he'd this one to deal with.'

"The fact is Miss, we're already finding cotton hard to come by. If this war goes on, we could be in the situation we were in 50 years ago during the American war, when there was no cotton at all. Never mind an outing, they'll be lucky if they get a bowl of soup, if it comes to that."

"What about a convalescent home for those who've become ill as a result of working for us?"

"Now isn't the time."

Evelyn wasn't convinced and decided the next time she spotted Becky, she'd go further into the idea. But she never did spot Becky. Weeks went by and she never spotted her, so she made enquiries.

"She's left, Miss," Barker, the chief clerk told her, looking quite pink.

"Left, where to?"

"Thought you might have known, Miss. Mr Shaw sent her up to Cara to put the house in order. Her family have gone too."

Barker was clearly agitated. Evelyn didn't know if it was just because he was answering to a female head, or whether there was something else.

Why would her father have sent Becky to Cara? There were surely women on the island who would have been more suitable. Becky was nobody's idea of a docile skivvy. Evelyn determined to question her mother at the earliest opportunity.

Doreen announced the Reverend Pomfret with her usual lack of deference:

"He's here again."

Esther didn't rise, but held out her hand and smiled beatifically. Pomfret seized it fervently and looked down on her, his eyes shining with compassion. He'd decided to accomplish his painful duty at once, but Esther forestalled him.

"I've seen Jack," she thrilled, "just now in the garden."

Pomfret was stunned. Had she lost her senses? How would this affect his plans? If she was considered insane, the estate would pass to the children. He'd no desire to be married to a penniless, mad woman.

"My dear, you're overwrought, quite understandably. The strain has all been too much. You must be mistaken…"

"Oh it was Jack alright. Jack bouncing about on the terrace. It was the way he cocked his head and gave me a cheeky look that gave him away. Then he started to sing."

Pomfret dropped her hand in dismay.

"Look there he is again," Esther cried. "Behind you. Look, quick, or you'll miss him."

Pomfret's scalp crawled. He didn't believe in ghosts of course, but what if…?

He turned apprehensively, and saw nothing. There was nothing but the French window. Then he did see something: a robin flitting boldly hither and thither. His heart resumed a more measured beat.

"Don't you see?" Esther cooed. "It's Jack come to say hello."

Pomfret perched on the edge of the chaise and took her hand in his again.

"It may be, dear lady. Who knows what wonders God can work, and if it is indeed he, he's come to prepare you for great sorrow."

His words had no impact. She smiled vaguely, but was intent on the robin. He squeezed her, hard until he had her attention.

Every line of his face, his very posture, suggested gravity. He managed a fleeting, but troubled smile. At last the effect he sought was produced and Esther's face became full of concern.

"My dear lady, I have not slept..."

"Oh I know just what that's like."

Pomfret held up his hand.

"Pray let me continue. This is a melancholy business and I'm anxious to have done with it, before my resolution fails me. As I say I have not slept these many nights. I have been wrestling with my conscience. I've heard, daily, the praises you've sung to your departed husband with anguish. I've heard the encomiums you've heaped on his memory and my heart has grown heavy. I have groaned inwardly at innocence abused, at trust betrayed. I have tormented myself Madam with this question: should I leave you with your illusions intact? Should I let you wander far from reality? Why should I of all people, who only wants your happiness, bring you sorrow?"

He paused here, squeezed her hand and looked tenderly upon her. He sighed and began again.

" I prayed to the Lord to show me the way. He answered my prayer and I knew I must open your eyes to the truth. The truth is a stern taskmaster. I serve the truth, Madam, and the truth commands me to speak. Be brave my dear lady. Be brave, as I know only one with such a noble heart can be."

He paused again. There were tears in his eyes.

"My dear lady, Jack was not the man we took him for. He had

another life. Oh I know full well he was more sinned against than sinning. I know full well that he fell foul of a coven of Irish tinkers. I know full well that it was the very innocence of his heart that made him such an easy dupe for their plots and machinations. He was no libertine, else they'd not have snared him so easily."

Pomfret paused again. The tears were overflowing. His voice cracked with emotion, but he forced himself to go on.

"Jack was unfaithful to you."

"No!" Esther's hands flew to her throat. The tears started to her own eyes. She looked down for her hankie. Pomfret observed her pink scalp through her snowy curls. She looked up again.

"Who? What woman?"

"Becky Flynn."

"Not her!"

"No, but she was the instigator of the plot I don't doubt. She came here."

"It's true. I saw her, but if not her, who?"

"A young relative, a niece, one who has sold her soul to the Devil in exchange for a dark gypsy beauty that could tempt many men less worldly than poor Jack."

"But what did she want? Why?"

"Blackmail."

"Blackmail!"

"Indeed, she blackmailed Jack to make provision in his will. And the poor man would have done so. He begged me to be a witness, but I refused. And yet when I found the poor man dead, there was the document on his desk, granting the fiends the right to live on Cara, and for the child..."

"The child!"

It was the coup de grace. Pomfret again paused for the right moment.

"His child," he intoned. "Of course I consigned it to the flames."

For a moment she just stared, open-mouthed. Then the shock ran through her like a bolt of lightning. Pomfret felt it himself. A deathly pallor shone through the powder on her face.

"No," she gasped.

For a moment he thought it might be too much, that she might drop dead at his feet, but she rose, tore her hand free and stepped involuntarily across the room.

"No," she moaned.

She turned and tottered towards the shrine and stared at Jack's photograph.

"No," she wailed. She saw for the first time the discomfort and embarrassment in his face and ascribed it to this awful thing.

"No," she screamed and swept photo, flowers, vases full of water, watch and pipe to the floor.

Pomfret acted decisively. He strode over and took her in his arms.

"Esther, Esther, let me bear the burden with you. Let me bear it for you. This may not be the time, but I can be silent no more. I've loved you with all my heart these many years. Let me care for you. Let me cherish you. Be my wife Esther. I know it's God's will that we should be together. Say you'll be my wife."

The big man shook with emotion and the tears gathered in his eyes. Esther said nothing. Had she heard? Had she understood? She suffered his embrace without protest though.

She broke away.

"Oh how could he?"

"Forgive him Madam. Forgive his weakness. The wretches laid a cunning snare. Forgive him. It may be the Lord permits him to return in the guise of our feathered friend, but if he does so, he comes to ask forgiveness."

He took her in his arms again.

Then she pulled away again.

"Get her off the island. Get her and the brat off the island!"

Pomfret held her by the shoulders. His whole frame shook with indignation. His cheeks flushed to think of such wickedness.

"I'll do it myself. I'll travel up there forthwith and cast them out. And if you'll let me, I'll devote my life to your service, to your well-being. No one will use you so again, or they'll answer to me."

He took her in his arms again. Esther said nothing, but she didn't resist.

Chapter Eighteen

Incalculable are the ways in which one life touches another. When Brigadier Horace Bradley, seventh Lord Hoddersdale carried out his inspection of the Lancashire Battalion, his gaze passed over Private Preston, seeing only another undersized example of a man who lacked the ramrod straight back and parade ground smartness of a professional soldier. Ben took more interest, having been taken for a poacher by his Lordship's gamekeepers only a few weeks before
   Majors and Captains followed. Among the former, Major Forrester, newly promoted for his zeal. Then came the Lieutenants, among these Nathanial and Peregrine. Peregrine recognised Ben as the solemn-faced lad from the counting house, but then many of the men were once employed at Empire Mill. Nathanial passed without a flicker of recognition, and neither were aware of what linked them, a link that would profoundly affect both their lives.

Bradley detected a lack of 'tone' in the battalion, an absence of any sense of urgency. He conceded this might be a result of the long wait for overseas drafting, a result of frustration, but he promised the wait would soon be over. They would be going to France. It was the 51st Highland Division that went first though.

Robbie sought Ben out with the news.

"Hey Ben, we're away."

"Where to?"

"Och you know the Army. Nobody's saying, but Billy Hamilton's giving odds on it's France, and he's not one to throw his money away."

Robbie had given Ben a beating, but had been immediately remorseful when he saw the lad motionless on the ground. He'd rushed for water to revive him and nobody had been more relieved when Ben had come round. He'd shaken him by the hand and called him a 'braw wee fighter.' Relations between the Highlanders and the Lancashires had been more cordial afterwards.

Some of Robbie's section joined him and there was much shaking of hands and slapping of backs.

"Are you going?" Dougie asked. "You lucky so and so's"

"Don't kill all the Fritzes," Yorky warned.

"Och we'll leave one or two for you to carve up," Robbie promised. "Keep your bayonet sharp."

"Don't you worry about that."

Colonel Scarlett had been a keen gardener. After long service in the east, he'd had Achaglass House built and, taking advantage of the climate warmed by the Gulf Stream, he'd planted palm trees and grown bougainvillea. There were more traditional blooms too. In late winter drifts of snowdrops appeared, where snow rarely lay. Later came the daffodils shivering in cold March breezes, and sometimes knocked out cold by sharp frosts. Then came the bluebells, the Scottish bluebells, creating a blue haze beneath the budding elms and beech trees, a blue enriched by the proliferation of forget-me-nots, a blue complemented by the purple lilac blossom that nodded above. With her time approaching Sadie liked to sit in the garden as the evenings lengthened, breathing in the fragrances, studying the play of light and shadows, but drawn time and again to narrow her gaze and look at the bright sea.

Tam had rushed up with the news of Jack's death.

"Terrible news. Terrible news. The Laird's passed away."

Though not unexpected, after Becky's premonition, it was a jarring reminder of mortality and the uncertainties of life.

"What will happen now?" Tam wondered, his staring eyes straining to penetrate the future. "His widow might sell, and then where will we be? We could be turned out of our homes. Such things have been known in the Highlands and Islands: whole families turned out into the snow, so rich folk can hunt deer."

"That's the system," Becky said, "the capitalist system. That's what we should be fighting, not the Germans."

It might not have seemed possible for Tam's eyes to widen further, but they did, and he wrung his hands and muttered prayers that the world should change so much that such terrible things could be said, and that it could be said there was much truth in them.

Nothing changed though. They were left in peace. On a wild April night, Sadie's labour began. There was no doctor on Cara, but with Becky, Rose, Mary and Meg there were enough women in attendance, and Tam did his bit, pacing the kitchen floor, ready to run down to the harbour to get Gus to row across for the doctor.

The fitful night gave way to a calm dawn and the baby was born as the rising sun turned the scores of raindrops on every leaf into diamonds.

Sadie held him, looking down on him, her lashes black against her pale cheeks.

"Well," Meg said. "I don't know what his father looks like, but he takes after his mother."

Becky thought she could see Jack in the pugnacious little face.

"You must have Robbie's christening gown," Meg said. "It's a beautiful thing, made by my grandmother on Skye."

"Oh I couldn't."

"Nonsense," exclaimed Tam, who'd been invited to join them. "It'll only be a loan. Robbie'll no doubt be wanting it back one day. He's sweet on Helen Macloud, who's away at the munitions just now."

"Have you thought what you'll call him," Mary asked.

"Ewart, I'm going to call him Ewart."

Tam clapped his hands and all but did a caper.

"A fine name, a braw name. Let's have a drink to celebrate." He looked at Becky. "Will I go and fetch a bottle from the cellar? I doubt the old Laird would have minded."

"Fetch two," Becky said and had no doubt that Jack wouldn't mind at all.

They were on their way. They packed up and shouldered their kit and marched down to Bedford Station. They might have been boarding a train to Blackpool, such was the excitement and high spirits. Ben sat with his section.

"I can't believe it. We're on our way at last," Dougie said.

"I won't blooming believe it till we get there." Smithy said. "We're heading south anyway."

Excitement fluttered only fitfully in Ben's breast. The passing of time, the drill and the discipline had ground the homesickness out of him. He'd bonded with his section. The battalion was his family now. But as the train rolled past the brickfields and the factories, bringing war ever nearer, he thought of Sadie. He'd written, but had had no reply. Was she better? He'd not dared to ask in his letters to Sally-Anne, but he was sure she'd have told him if there'd been any news. She told him about Evelyn running the mill: 'but then girls are driving trams these days,' and about Joe Wainwright being fetched up and fined for trespass: 'he should be doing his bit like you and it wouldn't have happened.'

They reached London. Not many of the men had seen London. Ben had never thought he would do. On and on it stretched in all directions: houses, shops, factories, warehouses, churches, streets, roads, bridges, endless panoramas in sunshine and shadow, losing detail and definition at the far horizon, where all blurred into indistinctness.

"The streets aren't paved with gold anyway," Pat observed as the train ran past grimy slums where barefoot urchins stood and stared.

"The River Thames," Yorky said, as they passed over the great, pewter river, "and there's Tower Bridge."

Green fields resumed as they rolled through Kent. The war was coming nearer. Would they be embarked by nightfall? Would they sail tonight, or have to wait for the tide? How long did it take to cross to France?

"Only a couple of hours," Yorky said, who knew everything.

They got no nearer to France that night than the cliff tops of Folkestone, where they were camped. They were to sail the following day. Some of the men went to look out to sea to the dark margin on the horizon that was France. There was a sound, a distant roar that faded and flared.

"Is that thunder?" Dougie asked.

"No lad," Sergeant Sutton replied. "That's the big guns in France. Somebody's getting a packet."

Chapter Nineteen

"What's the weather like?" That's what everybody wanted to know on the morning of embarkation.
Yorky stuck his head out of the tent.
 "Beautiful. It'll be as calm as a mill pond going over."
 Ben wasn't sure; the canvas sides of the tent were fair thrumming.
 Once again they got their kit together, heaved it onto their shoulders and marched off. Ben's feet and his boots were old comrades now and got on famously. It was a bright, breezy day. The Channel glittered. Gulls rode the air currents with the agility of monkeys swinging through trees.
 Folkestone folk had seen enough soldiers passing through. Only the very young and the simple-minded stared. The quayside was full of soldiers. A number of steamers towered above them.
 "I wonder which of those ruddy rust buckets we're on," Smithy

said, easing the weight of his pack with his thumbs.

"First time on a boat for me," said Pat.

"How did you get over from Ireland then, swim?" Yorky demanded.

"I was born in Liverpool, as well you know."

"I went on a steamer from Morecambe to Silverdale once," Dougie said.

"I've been on the Bridlington Belle more times than I can remember," Yorky boasted.

"Will we have cabins?" Nobby asked.

"Cabins!" Smithy said. "Who do you think you are blooming Jellicoe? We'll be lucky if we can sit down."

By now khaki streams were flowing up the gang planks. The NCOs were prodding and chivvying them into orderly queues.

As they shuffled nearer Ben's guts churned with apprehension. He could see now which boat their queue was leading to. He couldn't read its name yet, but as they got nearer still, he craned his neck and looked up the black, steel-rivetted cliff and read 'Duchess of Argyll.' The black paint had flaked off in places to reveal the red lead underneath. On or two sailors were leaning on the rail looking down.

'Alright for you,' Ben thought. 'You'll be back here, drinking in your local tonight.'

This was one of the momentous experiences of his life, embarking for a foreign country to go to war, and yet he felt detached, as though it were all passing him by, as though he were somehow missing the experience.

At last he was on the gang plank inching slowly upwards. Even the lower deck seemed a long way off. Would he ever come back? Would he ever mount a gang plank like this heading for home? By thinking he wouldn't might he be second-guessing Fate. Or does Fate always confound you? It was just such fretful speculation that divided him from the moment.

On deck at last, and there were soldiers everywhere. Their chatter, their laughter drowned out everything. Yorky shouldered the way towards the bow, where it was quieter.

"We want a good spot."

"Somewhere near a lifeboat," Smithy said.

"Will you shut up. I told you it'll be like a mill pond."

"Aye but what about submarines?" Dougie said.

"There'll be destroyers and cruisers looking out for us," Yorkie said.

They found a clear bit of deck, not far from the rail and sheltered by a bulkhead and dumped their kit. Then they waited and waited and waited. The morning passed. Some men stretched out and tried to sleep. Some wrote letters.

After noon Sergeant Sutton appeared.

"The Captain requests the pleasure of your company for lunch."

They all stared. He grinned.

"They're serving stew up in the galley, if you're interested."

He made to move on.

"Hey Sarge, when are we sailing?" Dougie asked.

"We might all be getting off and going back to camp yet. A U boat's been spotted."

This news was enough to curb most but not all appetites.

"I'm going," Yorkie said, rooting out his mess tin.

"I could manage a bit," Dougie said.

"Me too," Nobby said.

"Oh I might have known you would," Yorky said.

"Why not? We don't know when we'll eat again."

The others declined.

"Watch the kit you lot," Yorky warned. "There's some thieving so and so's about."

It was early afternoon before the crew's activity signalled something was about to happen at last. There was much dismal clanging from down below, a great deal of incomprehensible shouting, and suddenly the steel plates of the ship were vibrating to the rhythm of the distant engines. Smoke was coming out of the funnels. Fathoms of chain were being let out, or hauled in. There was the banging of gang planks being hauled in. Ropes were being deftly coiled. The quayside began to move away. There was cheering and the waving of caps. Ben didn't join in. He felt a lump in his throat. He stared at the rivets in the deck plates. They were blurred.

The whole harbour was moving away now. The gentle stirring of the ship on the water became more pronounced, became a decided rising and falling. They were on their way. Folkestone was receding. They were on their way to France.

With the coast of Kent falling away behind them, they got the full force of the pitch and toss of the sea. The steamer rolled and nosed down, rolled back and came up. Men who were standing had to hold on. Men who were sitting had to brace themselves first one way then another. Bits of kit began to slither about. Spray, like handfuls of jewels, was being flung over the rail onto the decks. Men were whooping and groaning.

"Some blooming mill pond," Smithy complained.

"Stop moaning. This is nowt," Yorky said.

Sergeant Sutton was going round.

"Keep your eyes on the horizon lads. Just keep looking at the horizon."

"Bit rough, in't it Sarge?" Dougie said.

"When you've been round the Horn a few times, you'll know what rough is."

"I just don't want to see that stew again," Dougie said. "I didn't like the look of it the first time."

Ben wedged himself as best he could, held on to his kit and stared at the horizon that was tilting and slipping, dropping and rising. He was mesmerised by the movement lulled. He'd feared feeling sick, but didn't do, exhilarated rather.

England was receding. The white cliffs were fading. Soon they were only a grey smudge on the restless horizon. There were other boats in sight, steamers, fishing boats and a yacht with taut canvas, flying before the wind. Where was he bound? Ben wondered. Could people be bent on pleasure, when all the world he knew of was caught up in the war?

The first men started being sick, retching over the rails.

"That's right lads," a cheerful sailor urged. "Get it up. Give the seagulls something to chew on."

And indeed the gulls were there, angling their wings to hang in the air alongside the ship.

"Did you see that?" Dougie shouted. "That gull's catching bits of the bloke's spew in mid air."

That was enough for Yorkie. He upped and lurched for the rail.

"That's right Yorkie," Dougie urged. "Give'em a good feed."

"First time I've seen him share his grub," Pat said.

The coast of England was gone They were in mid-channel, ploughing steadily through the lively sea. The Duchess of Argyll's wake arced away until lost in the welter of wind- stoked waves.

"I thought you were a good sailor," Pat said when Yorkie came back groaning.

"I am. I haven't been seasick. It were that stew. I thought it was a bit off."

"I'm alright," Nobby pointed out.

"I'm not surprised; you've a stomach like an ostrich," Yorky said.

On they sailed through the afternoon, and France was sighted at last. A grey smudge at first, but then a clear coastline, cliffs and beaches and white, foam-fringed rocks; French cliffs; French beaches and French white, foam-fringed rocks. The sea became less exuberant. Men lined the rails. The engines ran more slowly, with less urgency.

Individual buildings could be seen now - the buildings, ancient and modern of the port of Boulogne. The ship came to a halt altogether for a while, then crept into harbour at last.

Chains rattled; ropes were uncoiled; gangways run out. NCOs were bawling orders, getting the men into lines.

"Good luck lads," sailors said. "Give them Fritzes what for. Watch out for them French girls."

Ben was fascinated. Those men on the quayside securing ropes, or standing by watching were French. Knowing that gave them an exotic look. They seemed to have swagger and nonchalance. He couldn't hear their words for the hubbub of soldiers' chatter, but their every gesture betokened their difference, their Frenchness.

Down the gang-plank and he was on French soil. The very dockside cobbles were different. The buildings were different, more flamboyant. They had shutters at the windows and ornamental flourishes, balconies with ornate railings, roof tiles of unfamiliar design and colour.

The people were different, their clothing, their hair, the way they walked, the way they stood, the way they conversed. Ben was thrilled to hear his first snatch of French, utterly incomprehensible, utterly exotic. And how alluring the girls were. They swung along nonchalantly, aloof and lovely, utterly unattainable. One might glance and bestow, briefly, the flashing beauty of her dark eyes.

Many motor ambulances were crawling by at funereal speeds. Sergeant Sutton was marshalling the men into fours.

"There's a lot of ambulances Sarge," Dougie said.

"There's a big military hospital here."

"Why are they going so slowly?"

"They've got wounded from the front. Some of 'em's bad. Every jolt's agony."

They marched to the Gare Maritime. Many, many ambulances passed by. The streets seemed to be full of ambulances, all moving slowly, as slowly as hearses.

Chapter Twenty

Whenever possible new arrivals in France were put in a quiet bit of the front line with more experienced troops to get familiar with life in the trenches. The Lancashires were destined for the 2nd Army sector in Flanders where there were surviving regular army units from the BEF, in particular the Nottinghamshire Light Infantry.

The Lancashires had had an uncomfortable journey, travelling 40 men to a cattle truck, but at least the doors had been left open so they could admire the French countryside rolling by in the spring sunshine. The train had made frequent stops. On one such Arthur Kane from B Company, who'd worked on the railways showed them how to draw hot water off the engine, so they could have a brew.

Their destination was Cassel, a hill top town on the Flanders plain, home to the 2nd Army HQ in the former casino, overlooking the

Ypres salient, and from where you could see the North Sea. The men bivouacked in the barns and outbuilding of a farm by the station and next day marched towards the front line, twenty miles away.

They marched all day on a straight, level road, but the French cobbles were punishing. Poplar trees lined the route, their shadows like huge fingers pointing back the way they'd come, urging them to go back before it was too late. They came later to poplar trees that had been splintered by shell fire. They came to buildings too, shattered by shells. Every step was taking them nearer the German wire.

They reached the rear area by late afternoon, a chance for the men to dump their kit and smoke while the NCOs sorted out the arrangements. Ben's gaze was riveted by the sight of a dead horse that lay, unregarded by all, some distance away. It must have lain there some time, its flesh had sagged, the skin draping the bone. Yorky devined his thoughts.

"Takes some doing, burying a horse."

Sergeant Major Baker from the Notts Light Infantry came to address them. He was a regular soldier from the tips of his dusty boots to the top of his shapeless cap, that was pushed well back on his head. He had a moustache like a yard brush, sleepy, heavy-lidded eyes; with a fag-end permanently glued to his lip.

"Well me ducks, welcome to Duds' Corner. Just a couple of things before I shows you to your accommodation. When you get up there in the front line, don't go looking over the top to have a peep at Jerry. If any bit of you shows above the parapet, it'll get a bullet in it. We're nice and quiet here, but Mauser Bill won't allow liberties and nor will we neither. Secondly if you're on sentry go at night, don't go loosing off at shadows. We don't want Jerry to know he's got a lot of jittery raw recruits facing him, or he might get ideas. Right, now keep your heads down and follow me."

They dropped into a reserve trench and took the communication trench that led forward. Ben and Smithy happened to be right behind Sergeants Baker and Sutton, and could hear their conversation.

"What they like this lot then?"

"They'll be right enough. It's the officer you've to watch."

"Major Forrester?"

"Aye that's the one. He'll get us all killed."

"Thought so. He was talking to our CO." Baker put on a plummy accent. " 'I'm keen as mustard for my boys to put on a good show'. Looks like Major Mustard's got summat up his sleeve."

Ben and Smithy exchanged glances of foreboding.

They were heading east, creeping towards the night. Night seemed to flow down the trench. Night spread towards them from the front line, from the German front line. They were coming to the end of the known world. Beyond lay terror, chaos, annihilation.

They arrived at last into the front line trench. It was 'v' shaped with sandbags on the parapet and duck boards under foot. Here and there were fire-steps. Here and there was corrugated iron or timber shoring up the sides. Every few yards the trench angled away to minimise the effect of shells and to stop intruders machine-gunning all down the line. It was deep, but not deep enough for everyone.

"*You'll* have to keep your head down me duck," Sergeant Baker said to Nobby, who was a good six inches taller than anyone else.

"I'll have a crick in me neck," he squawked.

"Better than a bullet in your head, me ducks."

"You might not have much in there, son," Sergeant Sutton said, "but you might as well keep it where it is."

"Where do we sleep Sarge, in here?" Dougie asked parting the curtain of a dugout.

"No me duck that's for officers. You sleep out here."

"Here?"

"Well you can scrape a cosy billet in the side of the trench if you like. Anyway you won't be doing much sleeping, leastways not at night. Now who wants to see their first dead Jerry?"

Yorky didn't hang back. Sergeant Baker trained the periscope for him.

"Can you see him?"

"Bloody hell, aye. Why don't they get him and bury him?"

"They're not sentimental like us. Come on me duck." He gestured to Ben.

Ben squinted through the glass, seeing nothing at first but the dark wasteland, the broken ground, the vale of despair. The shadows were a meaningless jumble, but then he did see it: the bent knee, the raised arm; the body frozen in death. There was no head to be seen. It may have been drowned in the shadows. It may have lain some distance away. It may have been taken by the demons of Hell to gloat over. Ben's morbid speculation was interrupted.

"Come on, who's next? I should be charging tuppence a go."

Later the first of that night's flares went up - Verey lights shot up into the sky, illuminating no man's land with a brilliant white light for ten seconds or so, before descending and fading. Every few minutes one went up from one side or the other. Anybody out there had to freeze while the light endured, or come under fire.

"Who's going for the rum then me ducks?"

"This one," Sergeant Sutton said, pointing at Ben. "He's a Holy Joe, Band of Hope, Son of Temperance."

Sergeant Baker rubbed his hands.

"Right me duck. You've a job for life. Just you nip back down the line. You'll meet'em coming up."

Most of the activity in the front line was done at night. During the day, after the tense moments of 'stand to' at dawn; the most likely time for an attack, they got the chance to rest, to catch up on some sleep, to improve their bit of the trench. At night they worked; bringing up equipment and supplies from the rear; digging saps out into no man's land, which could be used as sniping or observation posts; repairing or putting out more barbed wire. They might venture further, nearer to the German line, their skin crawling, their breathing more laboured, as though the proximity of the enemy changed the very atmosphere. Here they would cut the German wire, or lie and listen, hoping to gather clues about the enemy's strength and deployment. Sometimes, rarely in this sector, there were raids.

Major Mustard was well named. Even in his pre-war territorial days he'd been keen, taking the 'Saturday night soldiering' very seriously, frequently clashing with subordinates, who were more casual, who failed to salute correctly, or failed to salute at all, in which case he'd have them on a charge. He'd never lacked belief in himself and his rapid promotion had only encouraged his confidence in his abilities. He was well aware of the low opinion the regular army had of the Territorials and he was determined to show them what his men could do. He explained his plan.

"Basically we're going to give Jerry a fright, give him a bloody nose. I'm going to take 20 of you chaps out there tonight, and we're going into his front trench. I won't say, don't take any prisoners, because we want some for interrogation, but I don't mind leaving a few dead on the ground. We'll grab maps, equipment, anything we can carry back. This is about morale, about keeping pressure on Jerry, above all about showing these Nottinghamshires that we're every bit as good as they are and a darned sight better."

There was a silence as Ben, Pat, Dougie, Smithy, Nobby and the others chosen to go contemplated the imminent prospect of death and danger. Lieutenant Peregrine Shaw spoke.

"The men haven't been in the front line long, sir. Maybe…"

Major Mustard cut him short. It gave him great satisfaction to be Peregrine's superior. Well established as the Forresters were in the Over Darren firmament, they were outshone by the Shaws. He certainly wasn't going to countenance an objection from a man who had condescended to him at social gatherings and had had the pick of the pretty girls at dances. Perry remembered Forrester at the High School, where he'd been an officious prefect, handing out detentions for latecomers.

Sergeant Sutton spoke too:

"Permission to leave Private Nobby behind, sir."

"Whatever for?"

"Well he's a big lad and a bit slow, if you take my meaning, sir, and…"

"Nonsense Sergeant. We want big men if we're hauling Jerry

prisoners back from their own front line. Have the men ready at 10.15 pm Lieutenant."

It was the Major's perceived shortcomings as much as their own that dismayed them.

"He's going to get us all blooming well killed," Smithy predicted.

"I'm looking out for myself," Dougie said. "I'll find a nice quiet shell hole and stick in it. Let him bag some Jerries if he wants to."

Nobby was indignant about almost being left out.

"What did the Sergeant mean, the cheeky sod?"

"He knows what you're like," Pat said. "He doesn't want you tripping over your big feet and giving the game away."

"I won't," he squeaked.

Yorky was nursing his bayonet.

"Can't wait to stick this into some Jerry's guts."

In the event he wasn't allowed to bring it, lest the flash of the bare metal give them away. They were encumbered with clubs, bombs, rifles and wire cutters. They blackened their faces with burnt cork. Ben's fingers shook. His breathing seemed no longer to be automatic. He had to remember to draw each laboured breath. He could not see beyond the moment of climbing out of the trench. He remembered the time he stood high up on the buttress all those years ago, about to leap into the void.

He was excused rum fatigue that night. Sergeant Baker came round dispensing the elixir and advice. He asked Ben.

"Sure you won't have a drop?"

Ben shook and shook his head.

The Sergeant massaged his shoulder.

"Have you a sweetheart me duck?"

Ben couldn't speak, just nodded, as an image of Sadie filled his mind.

"Well you hug the ground out there as though you was hugging her. When them Verey lights is up, don't move. Don't blink. Don't even breathe. There'll be a dozen Jerries with their rifles, ready to plug anything that moves. And don't forget your password. We don't want you getting shot by one of us, just when you think you're safe."

Major Mustard checked his compass bearing, checked his watch, whispered 'Follow me men.', climbed nimbly up the trench ladder and disappeared over the top. Lieutenant Shaw followed him and Sergeant Sutton after grim exchange of glances with Sergeant Baker went next. The men followed.

Ben's turn. His legs obeyed the message from his brain only shakily, but they obeyed and he climbed up the ladder. His head, his shoulders were above the parapet, in that zone where they might be perforated by bullets at any second. He pulled himself into no man's land by his elbows, slithered forward, following the boot soles of the man in front.

When the last man had gone, Sergeant Baker stood on the fire step and watched. Lance Corporal Darley joined him.

"Think they'll get back, Sarge?"

"Not all of 'em me duck."

The ground was cold and damp, but there'd been no rain for days. Ben feared the thudding of his heart would be heard by the Germans, or the chatter of his teeth. Bad as this was, he knew it could only get worse when they reached the German front line. Would he really be fighting hand to hand with German troops? He thought about what Dougie had said. Why not find a shell hole and sit it out, say he got lost?

They reached the gap in their own wire and began to crawl through. A Verey light went up. Ben pressed his cheek into cold earth, feeling the small, sharp stones digging into his skin. Even through closed eyelids, he saw the brilliant white light that was illuminating no man's land. Only when all was dark again did he continue.

Ahead were the shifting shadows of his comrades, the scrape of their boots. No man's land seemed so vast after the narrow trench, so exposed. Suddenly he was aware of noise and movement behind.

"Help," came the sibilant cry. "Help. I'm stuck."

Ben turned his head. Nobby was caught on the wire. He'd risen to his knees and was tugging frantically at his snagged tunic.

"Let go, you bugger!" he hissed.

A Verey light went up. All but Nobby froze.

"Freeze, freeze!" The word took shape in every throat. Every one of the 20 men hugging the mud out there willed him to freeze.

"Freeze me duck, freeze," Sergeant Baker whispered.

Nobby was intent on the wire, still tugging to free himself, glad of the sudden light on the situation.

"Why won't he be still?" the Lance Corporal demanded.

There was a sharp detonation in the still air, the silence was pierced, the echoes rolling away into the night causing faraway dogs to bark. The shock of the impact tore Nobby free of the wire, only for his body to slump back into its embrace and hang there.

"He'll be still now me duck," Sergeant Baker said softly.

Chapter Twenty One

Esther's sudden emergence from mourning into spring pastels and frills was not reassuring. Although Evelyn had been irritated at the extravagance of her grief, this sudden change did not bode well. Jack's shrine was gone. His photo was gone. Esther no longer referred to him. She was taking greater care of her appearance, forever consulting the mirror, making adjustments, rehearsing coquettish expressions. Evelyn wondered if she were losing her mind. She wasn't encouraged to expect a sensible reply to her question, but she put it nevertheless.

"Why did father send Becky Flynn and her family to Cara?"

Esther's new found frivolity was punctured, but only briefly.

"I'm not prepared to discuss it."

"It just seems an extraordinary thing to do. If he wanted staff he could have hired them on the island."

"They won't be there much longer, believe you me. Charles …Reverend Pomfret will soon send them packing."

"What's it got to do with him?"

"Everything. Everything has to do with him. I wasn't going to say anything yet, not until this business with those wretched women had been sorted out, but seeing as you know so much about it already, there can be no harm in telling you. Charles Pomfret and I are to be married."

There was nothing Esther could have said that would have shocked her daughter more. Evelyn stared, open-mouthed. There were so many things to say, she couldn't even begin.

"How can you…? What about Daddy…?"

"Your father's dead and buried."

"But not six months ago yet. The other day you were saying he was the finest man the world's ever seen."

"That's before I knew … That's before this business with these awful women."

"What business?"

"I'm not prepared to talk about that. Your father was a good man in many ways, but he was far from being an angel. Charles opened my eyes."

"What has he been saying about father?"

"I'm not prepared to discuss it."

"I refuse to believe Daddy can have done anything dishonourable."

"Believe what you like, but I'm not talking about it anymore. Charles is sorting all that out. All I need to do is concentrate on the wedding. They'll surely let the boys come home for it. They couldn't be so heartless as to stop them. I've high hopes that Lord Hoddersdale will attend. After all his daughter will be there of course."

All the while Evelyn was marshalling her arguments, choosing which would be the decisive blow, the one that would put an end to this folly.

"How old is Reverend Pomfret?"

"I've really no idea."

"Well let's say he's worn well, but even so he can be no more than 40, and how old are you mother, 65?"

"Not quite."

"Nevertheless, quite a gap. Doesn't that make you uncomfortable, suspicious even?"

"Why are you being so unpleasant? I thought you'd be pleased for me. I'm too young to spend the rest of my life alone."

The sheer grotesqueness of the idea robbed Evelyn of words. She felt it should be easy to drive home the utter folly of it, but words failed her.

"He's such a preposterous man."

"He's been very good to me over the years. Many's the day he's been the only company I've had, when you've been away getting up to all manner of nonsense, amusing yourselves with your silly notions. You especially Evelyn, all this nonsense about working at the mill."

"And why has he been so attentive, do you think?"

"Why, why, because he loves me."

Evelyn couldn't suppress an unladylike snort.

"Loves your money, you mean."

"You're not going to upset me. Charles warned me what you'd all be like. I'm going to write some letters."

Esther was too old and plump to flounce out of the room, but she did her best: she managed a dignified wobble.

Letters! Evelyn realised she too had some important letters to write.

The Reverend Charles Pomfret sat in his study and contemplated a rosy future. He gave full rein to his imagination. Things were going well. It hadn't mattered that he didn't have the will. Esther had consented to be his wife. That was the main thing. Once they were married, he was confident he could carry all before him, but if anything happened to prevent it, all was lost. Fortunately Perry and Nathan were away, but he well knew how Evelyn would react.

That's why he'd urged secrecy. The less time she had to make mischief the better.

Although he'd given Esther the impression that he would bring the wrath of God down on Sadie and her family, he'd no desire to have them back in Over Darren causing a scandal. He indulged himself by contemplating magnanimity. He'd give them adequate notice to quit. He'd no doubt a bit of kindness would have them eating out of his hand. He would even provide for them, when they eventually came back, after the wedding. He knew the master of the workhouse well and had good contacts with the local orphanage.

His pastoral duties would soon be nominal. He could employ curates. He would sell Ashleigh, when he moved into Woodlands. He could do nothing with Empire Mill yet, not while Perry had a majority share, but should the fortunes of war go against the young man… His plans for Cara were taking shape in his head. Clearing it of its inhabitants would be a necessary first step. He wanted people of his own choosing there, people he could command.

And then if Nathan's marriage went according to plan, another reason to avoid scandal, he'd have an introduction to Lord Hoddersdale's circle, one of the noblest families in the land, and what advantage might he not make of that, especially if had the hospitality of his own island to offer? Yes, the future looked good.

They were long silver days on Cara that May. The gold was seldom seen. The sun was behind the scenes, behind the clouds, lining them with silver and putting a sheen on the surface of the sea. Becky had roamed the island and met all who lived there. At Point Sands Farm in the south was McNair, a huge old fellow, a former Highland games wrestling champion, who now tended his few sheep, grew his few vegetables and was happy with his books and the chance to argue with occasional visitors.

Becky often called on Moira who lived alone and worked her handloom producing plaids that were sold in shops on the mainland. She showed Becky the working of it.

"It's good to tell you're a weaver," she said, admiring how quickly

Becky picked up the knack.

"I've sat at my Grandma's feet many an hour watching her at her hand-loom," Becky replied.

Moira kept cows too and produced some of the cheese the island was famous for. Becky wondered if there wasn't something here Ewart could be brought up to. Maybe he could learn to fish too. He could be independent, self-sufficient. Cara needed more people. Couldn't she rescue those who led ugly lives, take them out of the slums and bring them here?

Then came the letter that put all in doubt.

Tam raced up one morning.

"Will you look at the post you've got. All these for the young lassie. Will they be from her man? Och look they've the wrong address . They've had to be posted on. Why will that be I wonder? Does her man not know where she bides? There's one for you Becky. I chanced to glimpse the postmark. It's from Over Darren, and look at that hand. It's a lady's hand for sure. Will it be from the Laird's widow? Will it be telling us what she's a mind to do?"

Becky ignored him and passed Sadie her bundle of letters, then opened hers. Tam craned his neck to see and kept glancing back at Sadie. He was like a dog between two people eating biscuits, not knowing which was the best source of crumbs.

Evelyn had held nothing back. She'd written in a passion, careless of any indiscretion. Becky lowered the letter and stared. Tam hovered desperate for her verdict.

"Will you have a brew Tam? Put the kettle on Rose."

"They're from Ben," Sadie said. "He's been writing all this time and I haven't replied."

"Well now you can, " Becky said, still preoccupied.

Tam could wait no longer.

"Is it from them? Is it the Laird's widow? Does she say what she'll do?"

"No it's from her daughter."

"Nobby Clarke's been killed," Sadie said. "You know him. He used to live in Bright Street, a big boy, a bit simple."

130

Tam shook his head in sorrow.

"His people will be inconsolable."

Becky digested her letter's import.

It was clear the sanctimonious hypocrite Pomfret was after Jack's money. Why had Jack confided in him of all people? And what had he said to Esther to tarnish Jack's image so? She had her suspicions. She determined to write back at once and put Evelyn straight about Nathan's part in all this.

Tam was peering at the letter, his eyeballs all but curling over the edge of it.

"Tam, Tam! Go and get a cup of tea will you? If you must know, she's written to say we might be having a visit from the Reverend Pomfret."

Tam threw up his hands.

"Och, that one's a bird of ill omen, if ever I saw one."

"Well we must make sure he gets a warm welcome" Becky said," a very warm welcome."

Chapter Twenty Two

The Lancashires were out of line back at Cassel. Their mail reached them within a couple of days. Ben had a letter from Sadie. It said little, explained nothing, but it didn't have to. It was from her. Every word was precious. He wanted to be alone to read and re-read it. Both Perry and Nathan had letters from their mother. Perry had one from Evelyn too.

Major Forrester's trench raid had had to be abandoned. Firing had opened up on both sides and a German machine gun had begun a methodical sweeping up of no man's land. The raiding party had kept their heads down and managed to get back before dawn. The escapade did the Major no good at all in the eyes of the men, but his superiors thought it showed the right spirit, that it was 'a jolly good show.'

The next night they got Nobby back in off the wire. Rats had eaten his brain and where his head ended there was just an empty space.

"When I first saw this one 'ere," one of the burial party said, "I thought to myself yon's not got much in his noggin, and now we know I was right."

The others laughed grimly and dug their spades in, adding another plot to the cemetery growing behind the lines.

Nobby's death impressed the Lancashires with Death's efficiency, with its promptness and the swift attention it provided on the front line. It was hard for them to accept that Nobby was gone, that they would never see that huge, uncoordinated, pear-shaped body again, never see that lop-sided grin, or hear again that squawk of indignation, or suffer again one of his irrelevant interruptions to a conversation. It was as though they had been playing a game and he'd been sent off, or knocked out of the competition, and that they'd see him again later, that back home in Over Darren, they'd turn the corner of the street and see him, see his face light up with recognition.

Perry was dismayed by his Mother's letter and baffled by Evelyn's. Both bits of news came from completely unexpected directions, like being attacked on a flank that was thought well protected. What was his mother thinking of? Was her judgement clouded by grief? What could be done to stop it? The thought of the egregious Pomfret taking over Woodlands and threatening Empire Mill was intolerable. Evelyn said exactly that in her letter, but then how to understand the business of his father taking responsibility for the girl's child. He decided to consult with Nathan.

The HQ at Cassel in the old casino had a panoramic view towards Ypres. Preventing the Germans taking the town had become symbolic, an article of faith for the British. The Germans held the ridge that half encircled the town. They'd been able to reduce it to rubble with shell-fire.

The top brass could study their maps and then turn and look out towards the real thing. French, Haig, Smith-Dorrien were frequently there, as was Brigadier General Bradley, and the

Lieutenant Colonel of the Lancashires. Staff officer Lieutenant Nathan Shaw was kept busy dealing with all the paperwork that proliferated from the deliberations of the great war leaders.

"Oh I know what you think," he told Perry. "You think it's a cushy number here, but believe me twelve and fourteen hour days are not uncommon. It's rare for me to be in bed before two in the morning." Perry observed the opulent décor of the old casino, the deep carpets, the chandeliers, the Louis Quinze furnishings and thought of his dugout in the front line, thought of it shaking and lit up by shell fire. He thought of the rats and the lice and the smell of the dead. He smiled but said nothing.

Nathan took the chance to introduce him to his prospective father in law. The Brigadier General looked Perry up and down. With years of experience assessing men's potential, he saw at once that this one had more backbone than Nathan.

"I'm afraid you Lancashires are going to be in the thick of it soon," he announced. "We're making a big push to clear the Bosch from Hill 60."

"Very good sir."

"You've heard from Mother," Nathan said, when they were alone. "This marriage would be a disaster. What will Caroline's family think?"

"More to the point. What's Mother's life going to be like with that scoundrel, to say nothing of Evelyn's Has she written to you?"

Somehow Perry was not surprised to hear that she hadn't. He related the contents of her letter.

Nathan turned and stared out of the window at the town below.

"Queer business," he said in a queer voice. "I'll write to Mother and make clear my views about this marriage in no uncertain terms. And as for the idea of us taking leave to be there... Well even if we could..."

Perry knew he was concealing something, but didn't press him. Knowing he would be in action soon, he shook his brother's hand and looked him in the eye. Nathan's gaze fell away.

Nathan's thoughts were in turmoil. He was surprised that Sadie had confronted his father. She'd never threatened anything like that. In fact she'd said nothing at all that last time. She'd just sat there with the tears escaping down her cheeks from her thick eyelashes. He'd promised to do something for her, and had imagined himself doing so, had imagined himself installing her in a little cottage, whither he would go for discreet visits after he was married. He'd imagined himself making generous provision for the child, taking an interest in its education, providing suitable books, eventually finding him or her a situation at Empire Mill. He'd imagined it all and felt a glow of warm self-esteem at his generosity. He'd imagined it, but had done nothing, had left her weeping and had stolen away guiltily, just thankful to have avoided a scene.

The next time they should have met, Caroline had telephoned to say some of the motoring club gang were having a run through the Trough of Bowland with a champagne picnic to follow with the Burlingtons. Just the excuse he needed, impossible for any sane person to expect him to miss such a jaunt. The best people in the county would be there.

He'd still dreaded a scene, still dreaded her coming up to Woodlands. But as each month passed he felt safer. He decided in the end she must have dealt with it. Such people knew how to do these things. But then she must have turned up after all. Clever of the old boy to send her away to avoid any scandal, but why had he said nothing? And now he never would. Was he relieved that his father was safely dead? Did he feel stirrings of guilt? He worked late that night as usual, but the whisky bottle was never far away.

Poperhinge was the nearest town to the front line where normal life went on, though the occasional shell landed even there. There were estaminets where troops could get egg and chips and red wine or weak beer. There were shops selling lace and souvenirs. Later there would be the celebrated Toc H club open to all men regardless of rank.

The Lancashires were not there long. A fleet of London buses waited to take them nearer the front line. They were reminded of the trams at home and became animated and facetious.

"No point getting a return."

"I am. I'm staying on at the terminus and coming back."

"This'll never get up Whitehall Brow with all of us on."

"Standing room only."

"You should give up your seat, sonny and let an old man sit down."

The buses took them to Vlamertinghe and from there on they marched, and as they neared Ypres, the 'Gateway to Hell,' their high spirits subsided. 'The Gateway to Hell' it was called, but could Hell itself be any worse?

Not a building there was whole, not a building stood undamaged. Many had collapsed. Many tottered. Many reeled, shell-shocked. Always there was the sound of subsiding masonry, the dismal peal of shattered tiles, the crash of splintered glass. Shells still fell. Shells shrieked through the air – demons returning from their mischief and landing with a flourish of fire and brimstone, flinging up dust and smoke, pulverising stone and brick already pulverised a thousand times.

The black arches of a church stood defiant against the sky like the ribs of a great beast whose carcase had long ago been gnawed away by shot and shell. A thousand fires burned and the black smoke from them beribboned the sky as though Ypres had become a nightmare twin of Over Darren, where a myriad mill chimneys belched smoke and blackened the sky.

And there were people here. Many were dead and were occasionally reanimated by the returning demons, but there were living people too, people who took a chance and sheltered in the ruins, knowing a shell might cause the bricks and mortar above them to fly into the air at any moment, descend and entomb them.

The Lancasters marched through. The heat of the flames caused them to flinch. They marched past the ruined Cloth Hall, through the Grande Place where dead horses awaited the return of their demon riders. They marched through the choking smoke, marched over rubble and broken glass, marched through the Menin Gate, left the town and marched along the road to Hell itself.

Chapter Twenty Three

"Nathanial! I should have known."

Evelyn put Becky's letter down and stared out at the walled garden, where apple blossom was whirling giddily. Was this enough to make her Mother think again about marrying?

Esther was absorbed in the pages of wedding paraphernalia in the Army and Navy Stores catalogue.

"I've had a letter from Becky Flynn," Evelyn announced.

"That woman! How dare she write to us?"

"It seems Nathan's responsible for the poor girl's condition."

"Don't be ridiculous. Why would Nathan have anything to do with a creature like that? He's engaged to Caroline Bradley."

"Nathan's always been a fool where a pretty face is concerned. The point is the saintly Reverend Pomfret deliberately misled you, deliberately tried to discredit father for his own ends."

"I don't believe a word of it. I doubt the girl herself knows who the father is. They're just trying to take advantage of our good nature."

Evelyn didn't know whether her mother was deliberately not seeing the point, or was incapable of it.

"Can't you see what Pomfret's doing?"

"And can't you see that this is all your fault? You've been far too familiar with these people and now they think they can do anything. I knew no good would come of your silly notions, but do you listen to me? No, I'm just a silly old woman, who knows nothing, but I know one thing; Charles is a kind and devoted man and we'll be very happy together. Just because you can't find anybody yourself, you've no need to go spoiling things for others."

Evelyn didn't trust herself to speak. She left the room. She wasn't finished yet though. She was determined to confront Pomfret. She doubted she could thwart his plans, but she'd make him realise they knew what he was up to, that they weren't all fools.

She left the mill early and directed Dickens to stop at Ashleigh, a large Victorian gothic mansion with round headed windows and a steeply pitched roof. Pomfret's housekeeper was Jane Holden, who had had the drapers' shops in the High Street and on the Market, when her husband was alive. They'd both been prosperous members of the community, members of Pomfret's flock and he'd been glad of their patronage in his early days in Over Darren, and had been a frequent visitor. When her husband had died suddenly Pomfret had been Jane's prop and advisor. Shortly afterwards he left his modest vicarage and moved into Ashleigh, installing Jane as housekeeper, provoking much gossip among those with mischievous minds.

Jane was very quiet, very grave, very self-effacing. She was the kind of person who could enter a room and be there a long time before anybody noticed her. Only her hair was irrepressible, a reddish frizz. It seemed to have used up all her personality. She answered the door. She was dressed in decent black. Her pallid, rodent features twitched a little at the sight of Evelyn, but otherwise gave nothing away.

"I'd like to see Reverend Pomfret."

"He's with a gentleman."

"I'll wait."

Jane opened the door wider to admit her into the black and white tiled hall.

"I'll let him know you're here." Her voice had no expression.

Evelyn surveyed her gloomy surroundings. There was a hat-stand by the door with a few stout sticks. Stained glass at the bend in the stairs permitted a little light to filter down, and there was light from the door that stood open, whence issued the sound of male voices, otherwise all was shadow and confusion.

The voices grew louder. Pomfret and his visitor, Ephraim Neville, the town's librarian, came into the hall. Neville beamed at the sight of Evelyn.

"Miss Shaw! How very pleasant."

"Indeed," Pomfret echoed.

"I'm sorry to interrupt."

"Not at all. Your appearance could never be regarded as an intrusion," Neville said. He bowed and would have kissed her hand, had she accepted the offer of his own hand, which she did not. Neville was not abashed. What a catch Evelyn would be, a match made in heaven.

"I haven't seen you in the library for some time Miss Shaw." Evelyn made no answer. "If you can spare the time, I'd be happy to draw your attention to our recent acquisitions."

She inclined her head somewhat stiffly.

He bowed, took his hat from Jane and departed.

Pomfret showed Evelyn into the study. Sombre volumes were drawn up behind glass. Pomfret took refuge behind his desk, placed his finger tips together, watched and waited.

Evelyn dived straight in.

"Mr Pomfret I do not believe it is in my mother's interests to proceed with this marriage."

"You can scarcely expect me to agree."

"You would be doing her a kindness by postponing the arrangements for at least a year, and if she is still of the same mind then, I would have no objections."

"My dear lady, your mother and I are not children. We have our feet on the ground. Our heads are not in the clouds. We know perfectly well what we are doing. Your mother needs a companion. Someone to support her. Someone to lead her towards that eternal joy that is her due."

Evelyn switched her attack.

"I believe my father made some provision for Becky Flynn's niece.

Pomfret waved the notion away.

"According to Becky Flynn he did."

"And you'd trust to the word of such a woman?."

"I would ask you to recall what provision was made so that we can be sure to carry out Father's wishes."

"I doubt Esther would want that, and her wishes are paramount with me."

Aware of her impotence, aware she'd achieved nothing, Evelyn's temper flared.

"Don't think for a moment that we can't see through you. Don't think we don't realise it's Father's money you're in love with, not his widow."

Pomfret smiled benignly. He was relieved. He knew he'd nothing to fear.

"You're overwrought, and understandably so after all that's happened and with your endeavours to be a captain of industry as well. Take my advice and concentrate on helping Esther with our wedding arrangements."

"I certainly shall not. I won't even be there."

"Just as you please."

Evelyn flounced out, feeling she'd not done a bit of good.

Jane intercepted her.

"I can see myself out."

Jane fluttered after her, detained her in the gloomy porch and whispered with unwonted determination and urgency. Once she realised the import of her words, Evelyn listened intently.

The wedding took place on a fine summer Sunday. The moors above the town fairly glowed. The town's parks were radiant. Every tree was splendidly turned out. The flower beds were at their best. Black swans dipped their beaks at their shimmering reflections. The fountains sparkled. The grass gleamed.

The wedding attracted much interest. Crowds gathered to watch the carriage taking Pomfret and Neville to the church and the one ferrying Esther from Woodlands. Esther was touched, believing they'd turned out in their hundreds through loyalty and affection. However it was morbid fascination that drew many. They'd gathered to see Pomfret secure his prey.

Few boycotted the wedding. Nobody on Jack's side of the family had been invited anyway. The town's elite, however much they might tutt tutt, were not going to miss the spectacle, especially as they were going to be handsomely fed. Evelyn failed to carry out her threat, moved by loyalty to her mother and a desire to thwart the gossipers, who would gloat: 'even her own daughter wouldn't go!'

The vicar of St Jude's performed the ceremony. Pomfret himself cut a fine, manly figure in his top hat and tails. Esther thought he looked wonderful. She herself, a small, dumpy body in her confection of pastel net and satin couldn't help but look incongruous. She'd long ago lost the faculty of self-criticism however and saw the two of them as romantic figures, making a dignified and public profession of their mutual love.

The reception was at the White Hall Hotel. The gardens made a handsome setting for the photographs. The guests entered the dining hall via French windows. Pomfret spoke with his usual rotund eloquence, enumerating Esther's virtues, causing that good woman to blush and giggle and pretend to slap him. He modestly said nothing of his own.

As a man of learning and one who enjoyed any opportunity to air his erudition, Neville embellished his speech with literary flourishes. He cast Pomfret and Esther in the epic tradition of great lovers: Elouise and Abelard, Anthony and Cleopatra, Romeo and Juliet. He made flattering reference to Evelyn, which drew attention to her which she did not welcome. Then he read out the many cards and congratulations. Even as he did so a waiter proffered a silver tray.

"A telegram!"

He opened it with a flourish and was about to announce its contents. He never did. His whole demeanour underwent a remarkable transformation, as though suddenly deflated.

Seeking to rescue the situation, Pomfret took the telegram from him, read it and let it fall from his fingers. Before he could recover it, Evelyn had it in her hand.

She read, screamed and collapsed.

Chapter Twenty Four

"It's worse than Hell up there, mate."

"Good luck lads. You're bloody well going to need it."

"Fritz has got our measure alright, dropping Minnies right into the blooming trench. What's left of it."

These were the Gloucesters coming out of the front line, passing the Lancashires going up

Many said nothing. They stared, but saw nothing. Some gasped. Some tottered like frail old men. Some were wounded - white faces gashed with scarlet, field dressings stained red, hands dripping blood. It was a tight squeeze in the communication trench and some, despite the signs saying 'Dangerous Road. Use Trench,' climbed out and ran along bent double, risking the shells that screamed in, desperate just to get back.

Every detonation of every shell jarred every nerve in Ben's body.

He had no veto over his reactions, flinching and ducking at every explosion. In the front line the shelling was intense. The whining and shrilling became continuous. The detonations merged into a constant roar. The howling shells plunged deep into the earth and gleefully flung up armfuls of debris and shrapnel. Darkness flickered only fitfully in the infernal illuminations.

As in the weaving shed, it was impossible to hear what was said. The sergeants gestured, pushed and chivvied men down the trench. Ben led the way, stumbling along, head well down, bouncing off the trench sides, under a hail of stones and descending debris. His feet slithered on the duck-boards that floated at the bottom. Every few yards, he had to lurch in a new direction, following the zigzag of the trench.

The shells eased and when the ringing in his ears lessened, he could hear other sounds, the cries of the wounded in no man's land, the hoarse, urgent shouts of officers, and then to his horror, voices conversing in a guttural, incomprehensible tongue – Germans! Had Germans got into the trench?

He readied his rifle, braced himself for an assault. And then recognised words. Something clicked and he understood what they were saying. Not Germans, but Devonshire men. He'd made contact with the Devonshire regiment on the left flank.

"Fritz'll be over shortly," a stocky, stolid man informed him. "We'll give 'em a warm welcome."

He laid clips of ammunition along the sandbag at the top of the parapet. He had a methodical manner, seemed resilient and unmovable. It heartened Ben to be alongside such a man. He felt tears prick his eyes.

"You're Lancashires then. Where you from?"

"Over Darren, north of Manchester."

"Never heard of him. Still don't suppose you've heard of where I come from. Brixham it is, little fishing place. Your Lancashire's all factories and chimneys, isn't it?"

"No, you should see it now, well parts of it, like the Ribble valley near where I live. All the trees will be out and the grass growing and the hedgerows full of flowers."

"You hear that George", he said to his companion. "Lancashire here says they've trees and grass up there."

"Yes, all covered with soot though."

The two of them laughed. There was a companionable silence.

"When will he come, Jerry?" Ben asked.

"At dawn. There'll be five minutes of hate from their big guns and then they'll come. Bavarians they are over there, good fighters, not as bad as the Prussians. Saxons is what you want opposite you, then you'll get a nice quiet time. With a bit of luck Saxons might send over some sausage, especially if you lobs 'em some tins of bully beef. Don't suppose you've a cigarette on you?"

Even as a non smoker Ben always had a packet handy. They were distributed freely. He produced it and the Devonian became pally.

"What's your name? I'm Sam and this here's George. We'll just sit on the fire step and have a smoke. My head's big enough without lighting it up for Jerry to shoot at."

Ben squatted down with them.

"When will they bring some grub up?"

"Oh the waiter'll be along with the menu directly," Sam said.

George chuckled.

"It'll be bully and biscuits for the next few days. If we're lucky we might get a mouthful of hot tea. You got a girl at home, Ben?"

Conscious of the letter in his breast pocket over his heart, he nodded.

"You want to bring her down to Devon when all this is over, doesn't he Sam?"

"You want to come up to Over Darren and I'll show you the Ribble Valley."

"Aye when all this is over."

Ben stretched his legs as far as they would go.

"You be careful Ben," George warned. "If the Sergeant comes along with the rum and trips over your legs, you won't be very popular."

Despite the cold, despite the damp, despite the discomfort, Ben dozed. An image of his Father in Sergeant's uniform chasing him with a tablespoon full of rum popped into his head, then he was asleep.

Major Forrester went forward to reconnoitre the situation. On the right flank, at the point where they linked up with the Canadians was a series of derelict buildings out in no man's land. This was Sanctuary Farm and it was thought to be held by Germans. Major Forrester found it was actually empty and ordered A Company under the command of Lieutenant Shaw to occupy it.

The farmhouse roof had gone. Perry climbed the stairs and found the floor sound enough. Little remained to show of the lives of the family that had once lived there: the broken statuette of a saint; a shattered mirror; a corner table covered in plaster; the scattered leaves of a prayer book. The Germans had left empty sausage tins; cartridge cases; the ashes of the fires that had heated their rations.

Perry deployed his men and took a forward position himself behind a wall from where he could observe the German line. He was all too aware how exposed they were, in a mini salient in advance of their own line.

Ben woke from a deep sleep, from deep, troubled dreams. Awaking brought no relief. It was a little before dawn. A keen eye, one used to watching through the night might have detected an ebbing in the eastern sky, a dilution of the darkness. Ben was dismayed that he'd wasted the few hours, the only hours that might be left to him, asleep. He felt like a condemned man who'd meant to savour each minute of his last night, only to find he'd slept and the hour of his execution had come.

His bladder was bursting. He stirred, wondering which way the latrines were.

"Do it where you are," George advised. "Jerry'll be starting directly.

Ben was self-conscious still and wasn't sure he could do it, but when the first shell screamed out of the east, his bladder emptied swiftly enough.

The sound of that first explosion was like the starting up of the first loom in the weaving shed in the morning. Soon there were others, hundreds of them, thousands of them screaming into the earth, tearing out great chunks and spewing it with venom and fire at the cringing men. The ground shook. The very air shook. A torrent of dust and debris hammered down. Then the shelling stopped.

It was a while before the echoes died and other sounds could be heard.

"Stand ready boy," George said. "Here they are."

Ben took up his position on the fire step, and there they were indeed.

Coming out of the east in their field grey, like dawn itself, the Germans were advancing.

Ben suddenly knew this had happened before, perhaps in a dream, perhaps in a dream that very night, or in one ages past. He'd experienced this before. Part of him wanted to flee. Part of him was mesmerised. Part of him knew he had no decision to make.

The Germans surged forward, a grey tide that rippled over no man's land. Ben's heart thudded. His limbs shook. When would they open fire? Surely they shouldn't let them get any closer. He looked at Sam. The dawn light was in his face, but it illuminated no expression. There was a crackle of rifle fire further down the line and the urgent rattle of a machine gun. Bright red tracers stitched the grey layers of early mist.

A sound from above – the drone of an engine. There was a plane up, circling over no man's land.

"We'll be alright now," Sam yelled. "He'll bring the artillery down on'em. Best pot a few while we've the chance."

He took aim and began to fire.

Ben made his rifle snug and steady on the sandbag, zeroed the sight on a blurred figure in field grey and fired. Whether he hit him or not, he knew not. He worked the bolt and fired again, worked the bolt and fired again, fired again and again, fired in a frenzy at the incoming tide. He worked the bolt and fired again, and again, and again. By now shells were screaming over, tearing up the air, making no man's land heave and fall like the sea, engulfing the Germans in swirling eddies of fire and smoke, overwhelming them with waves of debris and flying spindrift of shrapnel.

Ben was on a beach, a long curving beach of dull white sand. The tide was on the ebb, listless, lace-edged waves unfurled. Behind him were dunes and clumps of spikey, grey-green grass. The sky was grey. Grey was the sea, and on the near horizon was the grey profile of a small island. A small island, with a hill at the south end, a hill cloaked with pine trees. A small island that was near enough for him to make out the harbour and the fishing boats that were moored there. Gulls skimmed the channel that separated him from the island. They keened and lamented.
Ben knew Sadie was there.

Chapter Twenty Five

The batteries of the Canadian and the Royal Field Artillery, directed by Royal Flying Corps squadrons had turned the tide, had turned no man's land into a sea of flying shrapnel and pounding high explosives. Men like Mick Moon of A Battery, 106 Brigade had worked their eighteen pounders to the limits, sending salvo after salvo until the muzzles had to be cooled with buckets of muddy water.

The German counter-attack had been beaten out. Only at Sanctuary Farm did they penetrate, gaining a toe hold and taking many British lives, Lieutenant Shaw's among them. Major Forrester led B and C companies in an attack which drove the Germans out.

Ben's conduct was widely admired. He'd climbed on to the parapet and, in full view of the enemy, had fired round after round.

His example had inspired his comrades. His reticence afterwards was put down to modesty, but in fact he had no recollection of his actions. There was a feeling that his courage should be recognised. Word got round and after stand-to Dougie, Smithy and Pat came down the line.

"Blooming hero," Smithy said.

"I can't remember anything about it," Ben admitted.

Dougie cocked a thumb in his direction.

"Red mist descending."

"You must have Viking blood," Pat said.

"Aye Ben the berserker," Dougie said and roared with laughter.

"Don't be saying that," Smithy warned, "or he'll get nowt. He's one of us and we deserve a gong."

"Well I did never see anything like it," Sam said. " He has a pee, climbs up on the parapet and starts blazing away as mad as a wopse. He must have sent 20 of 'em to their maker."

"50, more like," George said. "I lost count after 40."

"Hey, no be serious," Dougie said. "Don't you think he'll get summat?"

"Yes, confined to barracks for taking unnecessary risks," Sam said.

The Lancashires were pulled out of line and sent to the rear for a rest. Rest meant digging trenches, strengthening defences, carrying equipment up to the front. Ben's section was sent down to Poperinghe to pick up supplies.

Despite being near the front line and exposed to shell fire, the town went about its business as usual. Shops were open, cafes and estaminets were open. Old men sat over their liqueurs. Young women tilled the fields, and yet only a short distance away men were killing one another.

On the strength of many recommendations they sought out an estaminet called Madeleines. It was crowded with soldiers. They threaded their way through the smoke and chatter looking for seats.

"Pies hot! Pies hot!" a voice shouted above the din.

Ben looked and saw Mick Moon beckoning from a table. He approached with some misgivings, but saw at once that this was no longer the preening, cock-sure Mick Moon he remembered, but one worn and torn by months of fighting. Ben noted the stripe on his sleeve and the first class gun layer's badge above it. He'd always expected if he ever met him, he'd pass Mick Moon by with a distant nod, but he felt no animosity, no inferiority. It was a measure of how much he had changed too.

He went to sit down.

"Sit on the other side Ben. I'm deaf in that ear. Let me get you a beer."

"I don't drink, thanks."

"Well it's as weak as tap water. You could drink all night and feel about as merry as a wet weekend in Manchester. What I wouldn't give for a pint in the Mountain Eagle."

"You had any leave?"

"Leave! What's that?"

"You hear from anybody at home?"

"Only the missus."

Ben couldn't conceal his surprise.

"Yes I got married last year before getting posted."

"Who to?" Ben asked with a hammering heart.

"Rosie Smith. You know her. She was in our year at Church School."

Ben did know her, a plain dumpling of a girl.

"I didn't want to," Mick went on, "didn't want her to be stuck if I came back a cripple. Still look on the bright side, she might end up with a widow's pension."

"I had a letter from Sadie O'Donnell." Ben said. "She's living on that island of Jack Shaw's up in Scotland."

Mick snorted with indignation.

"So they've packed her away in some God forsaken spot have they? And I bet they've got her skivvying."

"Her mother and Becky Flynn are there too. She didn't explain why."

Mick stared at him.

"You don't know, do you?"

Bens shook his head.

Mick explained, telling him about Nathanial's betrayal.

"I'm sorry. I know you were keen on her. But now's your chance. They'll pay you to get her off their hands."

Ben said nothing. He just stared.

"Ben!" Mick shook him by the arm. "Ben!"

Three soldiers emerged from the press.

"This is where you've been hiding." It was Dougie. He recognised Mick. "Bloody hell, look who it is."

They all knew each other from school, or work, back in Over Darren.

"You're on a cushy number," Smithy said, "blooming miles behind the front line."

"You wouldn't say so if a shell lands on your ammunition dump, or one jams in the barrel and goes off, or if you have to manhandle an eighteen pounder into a gun pit through the mud."

Smithy didn't look convinced.

"What's up with Ben?" Dougie asked.

Mick told them he'd put Ben in the picture about Sadie

Dougie winced..

"Come on Ben. What's to do?"

Ben looked at him.

"Did you know?"

Dougie looked embarrassed.

"Aye we all knew, but we didn't want to say owt. We didn't want you upset."

"You want to get that bastard," Smithy said. "Put one in the back of his head when we go over the top."

"Not much chance of that," Dougie said. "The bastard's on the staff at GHQ."

"His brother's gone west," Pat said.

"*He* was a good bloke," Mick said. "He'd always speak when he passed your bench, ask if you were alright."

"It's always the good'uns that go," Pat said.

"I'll be alright then," Dougie said and roared with laughter. "What do you say Ben?"

Ben said nothing. In his mind he had Nathanial Shaw's head squarely in the sights of his rifle.

Chapter Twenty Six

Only officers' families were notified of their loved ones' deaths by telegram; other ranks were told by letter. By evil mischance the telegram notifying Esther of Perry's death had arrived with the wedding congratulations.

At first she was stripped of all falsehood, all pretence. Her soul stood revealed and she and Evelyn were at one in their grief. All too soon though, and encouraged by Pomfret, she reassumed her tragic role. She took centre stage again decked out in her extravagant mourning.

"We must bring him home. He must lie next to Jack."

Evelyn assured her this was not possible.

"But his brother's engaged to Lord Hoddersdale's daughter!"

Evelyn explained that soldiers' bodies were not returned, not even officers', not even those officers with prospective aristocratic in-laws.

"How would families who could not afford it feel, if they saw the sons of the wealthy brought home?"

"Well we'll have to go there. We must be at the funeral."

"Oh Mother, he'll already have been buried."

"Then we'll visit the grave. I'm his mother. The very least I can do is lay flowers on his grave."

Evelyn ignored the look and sad shake of the head Pomfret shot her behind Esther's back. She wasn't about to enter into any conspiracy with him.

"We will do Mother, but not now. When this dreadful war is over, we'll visit his grave."

"I'll have a tablet to his memory installed in church," Pomfret said.

Esther turned to him with tears in her eyes.

"Oh Charles, will you?"

He folded her plump, wrinkled hand in his manly one.

"I'll give instructions directly."

Evelyn wanted to say, 'what about all the other parishioners who've been killed?' but she let it go. She knew she'd lost her mother again and that her protestations would meet only with blank incomprehension and drive her further into Pomfret's power.

The plan to honeymoon on Cara was abandoned. While Esther was worshipping at the shrine to Peregrine, Pomfret began to make changes, began to roll out his plans.

From the proceeds of Ashleigh House he made generous donations to the Conservative Association and was adopted as a candidate for the forthcoming council elections, albeit in a ward represented by a Liberal, but he was confident. His star was rising. He was becoming one of Over Darren's public figures. He had momentum. His confidence was justified. He won the seat. He was later invited to sit on the bench as magistrate.

He was still disturbed at the number of young men of military age on the streets. He sat late at night in his study, formerly Jack's, with Ephraim Neville, using the town directory, voters' register and the library borrowers' records to compile a list of men who should be doing their bit. At the top of the list was Joe Wainwright, who still tramped the moors near Ashleigh in defiance. Both men agreed conscription was inevitable and they wanted to play major roles in the scheme when it came in.

He had no difficulty persuading Esther to sack Doreen and hire a butler and two maids, but servants were not easy to come by, with the high wages being paid in munitions factories. They found two girls Gillian and Anne, who were not entirely satisfactory, being young and slipshod, and, as it turned out later, already best friends. Barltropp the butler was an experienced man, but had been obliged to leave his previous situation on account of his advanced years. He proved rather slow and somewhat forgetful. Pomfret had deemed it wise to keep Jane close and had brought her in as cook/housekeeper.

He had a confidential interview with Old Hindle the family solicitor. He put it to him that he had a mind to replace Evelyn as Chairman of the Board. Old Hindle had reservations about Pomfret's abilities but was quite content to contemplate Evelyn's removal. Pomfret further enquired about the procedure for evicting Becky and co from Cara.

"There's nothing to say that Jack wanted them to be there?" Old Hindle enquired.

"Nothing at all," Pomfret replied.

All in all Pomfret was well pleased with how things were developing. Only one aspect soured his mood. He'd taken it for granted that the marriage was simple a union of his abilities and ambition and Esther's money and position; he had not envisaged a union of the flesh. Indeed he'd assumed they'd have different bedroom and that when they parted after dinner, they would not meet again until breakfast. Esther had other ideas. She and Jack had enjoyed physical intimacy right to the end. Esther was as much attracted to Pomfret because he was a fine figure of a man as she was by his intellectual qualities. She was quite adamant that they share the same bed. Pomfret did not look forward to bedtime.

There was something else he'd discovered about Esther: beneath the fluff and froth was pure steel. She rarely troubled to show it, but Pomfret knew if it ever came to a clash of wills; she would prevail. He knew he'd just have to manage her, manouevre her, avoid a confrontation.

Evelyn too paid a visit to Old Hindle. When she'd been waylaid by Jane after the interview with Pomfret, the woman had told her that she'd chanced to see a document on Pomfret's desk relating to the settlement of Cara on Becky's nephew.

"Would you swear to its contents in court?" Evelyn had asked.

Jane had shrunk in alarm

"Oh I don't know Miss. I can't say," she'd whispered almost inaudibly and had faded away.

Evelyn's question to Old Hindle was:

"Would statements to the effect that my father intended Cara to be home for his illegitimate grandchild have any legal effect?"

Old Hindle's expression was habitually mournful. He seldom smiled and it was bad news for somebody if he did. He rested his melancholy gaze on Evelyn's face.

"Who would be making these statements?!

"My mother and Jane Holden, Reverend Pomfret's housekeeper, and possibly the Reverend gentleman himself."

"Reverend Pomfret has seen such a document?"

"He may have it in his possession."

Old Hindle weighed this against Pomfret's query on the same subject. There was something here, some subterfuge, some skulduggery. He looked down in case the interest the news caused him should show in his eyes.

"The decision as to who may or may not live there is in your Mother's hands anyway."

"Yes, but if she declines to act, would the fact that the document had been seen and attested to have any legal weight."

"Reverend Pomfret would so swear?"

"Probably not."

"Just his housekeeper's word then." Old Hindle shook his head. "The case might line the pockets of a good many members of my profession, but I fear it would come to nothing."

After Evelyn had left, Old Hindle contemplated the situation with his fingers laced across his fancy waistcoat. Pomfret was a rogue, he was quite sure of that and he admired him all the more for it, nevertheless he'd been family solicitor to the Shaws for many years, and his duty and loyalty were to them. For the moment nothing was to be done, but he would be following the career of the Reverend Charles Pomfret with close interest.

Evelyn wrote to tell Becky about Perry's death. Becky sent back her condolences. She said Ewart was thriving, playing in the sand on the beach, that the garden was in bloom and the island looking lovely. In answer to Evelyn's query about what could be done for the workers at Empire Mill, Becky said she was more convinced than ever that Achaglass House would make a wonderful convalescent and rest home for injured and sick workers. It was a suggestion that had already taken root in Evelyn's mind.

Lieutenant Nathanial Shaw had requested an interview with Brigadier Bradley. The Brigadier could see a change in the young man. He was pale. His features were finely drawn.

"I was sorry to hear of the death of your brother."

"Yes sir."

"He was a fine man and died a brave death."

"Yes sir, thank you sir. I want to replace him."

He had not expected to hear this. It pleased him. The young man had gone up in his estimation, almost to the point of being worthy of his daughter's hand. He decided to test his resolve a little.

"You're a good staff officer. You're more use to me here."

"I'm sorry sir, but I feel it is my duty."

"And if I refuse?"

"Then I would resign my commission and re-enlist as a private, sir."

"And resign all hopes of marrying my daughter too?"

"I'd hope to make myself worthy sir."

"And I'm sure you would do, but it won't be necessary. Your

request is granted. You'll be with the battalion in time for the big push this autumn."

"Yes sir. Thank you sir."

Lieutenant Shaw saluted smartly, turned about and left.

Chapter Twenty Seven

The autumn rains came early to France and Flanders. For days on end it rained and whenever shelling died down, it could be heard, thundering on corrugated iron, sizzling on cobbled roads, pattering on canvas, whispering on mud, sighing on swamps and flashes of foul water. It dripped from men's waterproofs, from the peaks of their caps, from their noses. They were days on end in wet clothes. They stood in water knee deep, thigh-deep in the trenches.

Beyond the Menin Gate was a forsaken sea of desolation. Whole villages such as Zonnebeke, had been flattened, obliterated, lost in the sea of grey mud. Grey water, grey mud, grey skies and the rain slanting down, with the flash and smoke of exploding shells, that was all there was. Across this landscape the Division had to go.

Just outside Ypres was Hellfire Corner, a crossroads and one of the most shelled areas on the front. Canvas screens had been put up to hide the moving column from the Germans, but the shells still screamed in.

The Zonnebeke road ran through a cratered landscape. Every crater brimmed with deliquescent mud, stagnant water, tainted with gas, cordite and decomposed flesh. Many craters ran together to form lakes. River banks had been reduced by shellfire; drains had been pulverised. The water had spread to form small seas and where the water couldn't reach there was mud, malevolent mud, predatory mud, mud that if it could once seize a man by the ankle would pull him in. If he was quick or lucky he might escape by sacrificing a boot, but if the mud got a purchase on his leg, he was gone. Weighed down by 60 pounds of equipment, he had no chance of getting out unaided, and anybody who offered a rifle butt to the drowning man risked being pulled in too. In many a crater bodies could be seen clinging to rifles that had been skewered into the mud by the bayonet by men hoping to cling on until rescued, but rescue never came.

Artillery had to be moved up too, sixteen pounders, each gun pulled by a team of six horses. The road out of Ypres was solid with army service lorries and wagons, gun limbers and infantry moving slowly forward. On either side of the road was the mud that would swallow a gun and its horses as eagerly as an infantryman and his equipment. And into this mass shells would plunge, driving hot shrapnel through men and beasts, causing a chaos of screaming horses and smashed transports. And still it rained.

Ben and his section were moving up too, hemmed in by wagons, horses and lorries. They were soaked to the skin, shaking with cold and fear. It seemed impossible to imagine it getting worse, and yet if they were hit by flying shrapnel, or a panicking horse drove them off the road into the mud, it would soon be very much worse. And at the end of it, at their destination, they would be going into the attack. They would be going over the top, going over the top for the first time.

The timetable for the attack had slipped and slithered and was now as irrecoverable as anything that had fallen prey to the mud. It was late afternoon and the Lancashires should have been taking their first objectives. Mick Moon's battery should have been sending over a protective barrage, but had still not reached its allotted position.

Ben staggered under the weight of his equipment. He was hung about with spade, mills bombs, bandoliers of spare ammunition, water bottle, box respirator, two day's rations. They might have been nailed to him for the pain they caused dragging and swinging, pulling him off balance, putting him off his stride. Only his rifle weighed nothing. His rifle was part of him.

Marching four abreast was impossible, three abreast, two abreast was impossible. It was impossible to march. Men just staggered along, trying to keep out of the way of the wagons and the horses. Smithy came up behind Ben and put a hand on his shoulder.

"Seen anything of Sutty?" he asked, mouth open, gasping.

Ben hadn't seen the sergeant. He shook his head, sending water droplets flying.

"Give us them bombs then."

"I can manage."

"Give 'em here. I'm not going to carry 'em."

Ben unslung the six mills bombs. Smithy took them, glanced behind him, stepped to the edge and dropped them into the mud.

"Give us your shovel."

That went the same way.

"You'll get on a bit better now, and guess what I've heard - Lieutenant Romeo's been winkled out of HQ and has taken over A company."

This opened up a new avenue for Ben's thoughts and for a while the fatigue, the pain, the fear receded. By now wounded were coming down the road, compounding the congestion. Dougie and Yorky walking together found themselves in the path of a motor ambulance. Behind the rain-swept windscreen the driver was invisible.

"Mind my foot," Dougie yelled and banged on the door as it swept them aside.

"Let 'em run over it," Yorky said. "You can get in the back then, a nice blighty one."

As it lurched past they heard the groans and curses of those inside, and the rain running off it had a crimson hue.

Mick's battery officer was Lieutenant Miller, known as Birdy as much for his beaky nose, bright button eyes and darting manner as for his interest in ornithology. The guns should have been in position hours before, but progress up the Zonnebeke road had been fitful, long periods of immobility with painfully slow progress in between.

The screech and shatter of incoming shells caused the horses to rear and plunge and go rigid with terror, until only cruel whipping would move them on. The spot marked on the map for the guns proved impossible: deep mud, covered with water. There was firmer ground in the ruins of Zonnebeke village. They manhandled the guns off the road and made platforms with salvaged bricks. The only protection the men had were the shields of the guns themselves. Mud soon jammed the breeches and they had to use pick axe handles to force them open, but at least they were in position and firing, sending some sort of reply to the German shelling. The recoil of the guns forced them back into the mud and made accurate fire impossible. The mud had one advantage, incoming shells buried themselves deeply and their impact was muted.

For a time the chaos on the road seemed beyond all resolution. For a time there was a complete standstill. The wounded going down and the men coming up were deadlocked, milling about, unable to disentangle themselves. To the wounded in agony, it seemed their torment would never end, that the unbearable pain that gripped them so fiercely would never relent, only get worse. For the men going up, weighed down with equipment and water-logged clothes, there gleamed the hope that they might never get there, might never reach the front, might never have to go over the top.

But the knots unravelled. The chaos disintegrated. The dogged persistence of officers and NCOs prevailed. The wounded reached casualty clearing stations and thence to whatever lay ahead: death or the slow road to recovery, and the men going up began to see there was no escape. Their fate would be decided in no man's land. They would be going over the top.

There were flashes of fire and plumes of black smoke up ahead. The roar of exploding shells rolled back over their heads. Ben and Smithy were too weary to react. They plodded on, mouths agape, catching rainwater on their parched tongues. Sometimes they collided and stumbled. Ben wondered how long his will power would prevail. He was fired by the knowledge that Lieutenant Shaw was somewhere nearby, up ahead or just behind. He wasn't going to falter and fall out in his presence, but how long could he continue with the dead dragging weight of his equipment, the deathly embrace of his sodden clothes, and the agony of his bruised and blistered feet?

It was growing dark by the time the Lancashire Battalion reached the reserve trench. The day's battle plan had been abandoned. Before nightfall the battalion should have reached the green line behind St Julien and Frezenberg. Revised orders had come through that the Lancashires should attack as soon as they reached the front line, but their Lieutenant Colonel had come forward on his grey horse and seen the condition of his men. They'd been on the move since the night before. They'd had no sleep for over 24 hours, no food for over 24 hours. Facing them were experienced German troops in well fortified positions. The guns which had been supposed to soften up these defences and cut the wire were barely yet in position. He was not hopeful that the position would be much improved by morning, but at least the men would have had a rest. He sent a messenger back with the word that the Lancashires would attack at dawn.

Chapter Twenty Eight

Brigadier General Bradley studied the maps again, then walked over to the window and looked towards Ypres and beyond that shattered city to the Hoog salient where the battle would be fought.

With good luck and a fair wind there had been a slim chance of success. They outnumbered the Germans by seven to one, but the Germans were well dug in behind extensive wire in three lines of defence. The Germans had learned of the attack and had plastered the Menin road with shells. The fair wind had not materialised, but the foul wind had, bringing heavy, incessant rain that had turned the whole salient into a sea of mud.

This wasn't warfare. No general would have contemplated an attack over such ground. Bradley had counselled against it himself. This was politics. It was necessary to prove to the French that the British meant business and for that reason and that reason alone thousands of men would die and thousands more would be wounded and not a yard of ground would be gained.

The Lancashire Battalion would be in the thick of it. Bradley found himself contemplating Lieutenant Shaw's fate. As a junior officer with no battle experience his chances of surviving were practically nil. He could have kept him out of it. What would Caroline think? He turned away from the window.

The girl would get over it. The match had not been suitable anyway. He'd not been fool enough to forbid it, but he'd not approved. He remembered the one meeting he'd had with the man's father, the mill-owning chappie – frightful fellow, no idea how to behave in society, and his wife had been even worse, a perfectly ridiculous creature. No, the family could do without that kind of blood.

He thought of his own son and his heart warmed. There was a man for you. There was a soldier. He was a captain in the Horse Guards, a perfectly splendid chap, excellent horseman. The other fellow couldn't even sit on a horse. Rupert was widely admired by his fellow officers, hugely popular. A better catch for Caroline could surely be found amongst Rupert's friends.

And yet, and yet, what character Shaw had shown. He might have seen the war out in safety. When 2nd Lieutenant Ponsonby, Shaw's replacement, brought a communication. Bradley vented some of his dissatisfaction and sent the young fellow away with his cheeks burning.

The men were so cold, so wet, so weary, so miserable that for many a bullet through the head would have been a blessing. Ben shivered uncontrollably. It was midnight. Out in no man's land the star shells ignited the slanting rain and made the dead man's face in the trench wall opposite glow. They were going over at 4.00. Ben was standing in water up to his knees. The bones of his feet and legs ached. He shook and shook and if he unclenched his jaw, his teeth chattered. He could no longer tell, without looking, whether he held his rifle or not. He could still feel the sore grooves in his shoulders worn by the straps of his equipment, and he could feel the damp of the trench wall against his back, even through his wet coat. And yet despite all this, his eyelids drooped and absurd fancies flourished in his mind.

He could hear the Jocks talking.

"We were in a trench one time and there was the hand of a Fritz sticking out of the wall. We had a right bastard of a Sergeant called Mackay, and every morning he came down the line, shook this hand and said 'Morning Fritz.' One night we dug Fritz out and Jocky Wilson got in there and stuck his hand out. Mackay comes down as usual, grabs the hand, but before he can speak, Jocky squeezes it for all his worth."

They all laughed.

"What happened to Mackay?"

"Oh he was up and over the back of the trench as though a Minnie had gone off under his arse."

"Two hours to go lads. Two hours to go lads." The words woke Ben. The Sergeant was coming down the line.

"Two hours to go and I'll be blooming well dead, or wish I was," Smithy muttered.

Ben hadn't realised he was there. He looked the other way and there was Dougie. Where were the Jocks? Had they really been there? He dozed again.

"One hour to go lads. One hour and you'll be hanging on the old barbed wire."

Had the Sergeant really said that?

"Ee, this is grand." Dougie said, turning his dripping face towards him and roaring with silent laughter. Those were the last words Ben ever heard him say.

"Thirty minutes to go lads, thirty minutes."

The trench ladders were being installed. The activity sent waves lapping round Ben's thighs.

It was early morning in the weaving shed. The looms were standing up to their warps in water. Ben's grandfather Cuthbert was standing waist deep, arms akimbo surveying the situation.

"Fifteen minutes lads, fifteen minutes."

Ben roused himself. He stood his rifle down and clenched and unclenched his hand until he had enough feeling to be able to undo the cover that protected his rifle from the mud.

Terror was now driving all else from his mind. He no longer felt the cold, the damp, the aches and the pains. He felt only fear.

"Five minutes lads, five minutes."

Men began to queue by the ladders. There was a lot of splashing, a lot of curses, whispered prayers, desperate jokes.

"One minute, one minute."

That minute lasted an hour. Ben counted the 60 seconds half a dozen times, and still the minute endured, still they waited. Maybe the attack had been cancelled. Maybe time had stood ...

Whistles blew far and near blasting the still of the night at its most vulnerable moment, alarming the watchers of the dawn, alarming the Germans too who looked to their defences.

The men began climbing the ladders. The first ones got out into no man's land, but by the time the second ones were emerging, the machine guns had started. Dougie was hit while still on the ladder. Ben heard the bullets strike home. Dougie fell back with a hollow splash into the bottom of the trench.

"Leave him, leave him," shouted the Sergeant. "It's only a scratch. He'll be on is way to Blighty. Keep going."

Ben climbed the ladder knowing Dougie wasn't going home to Blighty; he was going home to meet his maker.

The wire sang and blue sparks flew where the bullets struck it. The Germans had registered on the gaps where the men were queuing to pass, queuing to be shot.

Ben was braced against the lurching weight of his equipment and the clammy hug of his sodden clothes. He kept clear of the sheets of water, not knowing how deep they were. The mud detained him, clinging to his boots or causing him to slip. An officer passed and ordered him to keep up. A star shell burst illuminating his bone-white face. Did he recognise him? Was it Lieutenant Shaw?

The figure had gone on into shadow before he could be sure.

Machine guns gibbered incessantly. They levelled the first wave, then began to thin out the second.

Shells screamed in rearranging the way ahead, shaking the ground, spewing oily smoke, red and orange fire. Red hot shrapnel scythed through flesh and bone and suffused the driving rain with crimson. Red hot shrapnel flew into the many stagnant pools. Steam billowed.

Ben no longer knew which way was forward and which way was back. A shell blasted him off his feet and as the earth tumbled around him, he no longer knew which way was down and which way was up. The roaring of successive explosions was underpinned by the inane chatter of machine guns. Nothing was still. Mud and water leapt and danced all around him. The ground shook again. The air shook. Shell after shell detonated dismantling the men the machine guns had overlooked. An inferno of fire and smoke raged around him and out of it came a head screaming and trailing flames. And though it was more glowing, grinning skull than face, Ben knew it was Smithy's head and it hit him beneath his left eye.

The boat ran up on to the beach, the keel biting on the wet sand. Ben stepped out and pulled it clear of the gentle ripples. This was the island. The sky was a fine blue, with skeins of cloud stretched to gossamer. The beach was a white crescent between the calm blue sea and the fringe of pebble and driftwood by the sand dunes. A stream ran across the beach. Oyster catchers and dunlin prodded about in the shallows.

Ben walked up the beach.

Chapter Twenty Nine

Like many men Pomfret discovered that his wife did not behave as anticipated before marriage. She was not spineless, not empty headed. Any attempt on his part to exert authority would be met by her withdrawing into a private world, by her becoming vague and unreachable. She would smile sweetly, if he attempted to thunder. She was perfectly aware of her position, of her advantage over him. She knew he could not act without her concurrence.

To his dismay Pomfret soon discovered that she was at her most compliant in the marital bed, that when she was snuggled up in his arms in post-coital bliss, she was most likely to agree to anything he proposed. Thus at the very moment when what he wanted most of all was to turn his back and distance himself, seek refuge in the furthest corner of the bed, he had to hug her, hug her shapeless, yielding form closely to him, as though she were the dearest thing in his life. It was on just such an occasion when he proposed supplanting Evelyn on the board of Empire Mill.

"Of course you must Charles," she whispered lifting her face for the kiss he could not avoid bestowing. "Why Jack agreed to it is beyond me."

"His judgement was not always sound."

Esther had got into the way of rebutting his criticisms of Jack, but she let that one go.

"I will speak to her tomorrow."

"Of course you must."

"And you'll support me."

"Of course I will."

Pomfret made to move.

"Don't turn over yet Baby Blue Eyes. Mummy wants a long cuddle."

Groaning inwardly, Pomfret hugged her close.

Evelyn flamed with indignation when Pomfret made his announcement in the morning room after breakfast.

"What do you know about running a mill?"

"I might question your own knowledge on that head," Pomfret replied, "but I know what's in men's hearts, or rather what should be. I will see to their spiritual welfare."

"It's their material needs that must be addressed first."

Evelyn was especially vexed, having found at last something she could do for the workers. Exchanging letters with Becky they'd both agreed on the idea of opening a convalescent home on Cara. She'd not put the plan to the Board yet, anxious to have details and financial figures to hand, knowing there'd be opposition.

Evelyn looked to her mother, who sat serene and composed, in her mourning still, black ribbons in her snowy hair. Evelyn knew there was nothing to be hoped for from her, but made the attempt anyway.

"And what do you say mother?"

"I agree with Charles of course. I always was opposed to you working there, hardly a suitable place for a lady."

"We don't know Nathan's views," Evelyn pointed out.

"I'm rather of the opinion that he thinks as we do," Pomfret said, "but even if he does not Peregrine's shares have reverted to your mother and she now has a majority holding. Of course I would have no objections to you attending meetings, until Nathanial returns anyway."

His monumental effrontery put Evelyn in a rage. She wanted to rush over and rake red trails in his smug face with her nails. She turned and left.

Pomfret never had the need to order the Jezebels out of paradise in person; a letter, which he dictated to Esther, sufficed.

"We've got our marching orders," Becky said, reading the letter from Esther. "I can remember when Esther Shaw ran about with no shoes on her feet, now listen to her: 'You are required to vacate on receipt of this and leave Achaglass House in a clean and tidy condition.' Of course that'll be him. All she could ever do at school was draw fairies on her slate."

Hamish was peering, desperately trying to read the letter upside down. Becky handed it to him. Ewart started crying. Sadie picked him up out of the drawer they were using as a cot.

Becky crowed over him and tickled his tummy.

"You're going home Ewart."

Sadie shook her head.

"No, he isn't. This is home."

"Well said, Lassie," Tam said. "He was born on the island. Nobody can take that away from him, however many poonds they have in the bank. He'll always be a Highlander."

There was little to pack, but many farewells to make. Hamish hugged her and growled.

"If I was ten years younger, I'd ask you to marry me."

"If you were 50 years younger, I might say yes," Becky said, pushed him away and slapped him.

Moira was composed. She bade them all farewell with an embrace, but said.

"You'll be back, I know it. Cara will call you back. Just wait and see."

Tam and his wife were more demonstrative, both brimming with tears.

"It'll be us next for sure," Tam said. "They'll have us off the isle, I've no doubt about it."

"Come down to Lancashire," Becky said. "There's plenty of work.

"It'd break our hearts to leave," his wife said. They clasped hands and regarded each other. They were mirror images of misery.

Sadie made no complaint, accepted her fate, but as they left in the steamer, she stood at the stern and looked back at the island, and there were tears in her eyes. Becky was looking forward to parading Ewart through Over Darren, naming the father to anybody who asked.

It was when he presided at the Military Service Tribunal that Pomfret was in his pomp. With his fellow councillors and with the police in attendance to haul away the recalcitrant, and with an audience of public-spirited townsfolk, he felt he was assuming something of the status that was his due. He felt more than ever that in this role he was carrying out God's will. He was not made of stone. He was not without feeling. He was not unmoved by some of the tales of hardship, but he knew where his duty lay. Almost as if he had seen the men mown down in their thousands, he knew that God's work would not be accomplished without more men, men in their thousands, men in their tens of thousands, men in their hundreds of thousands. Businesses would have to close if need be. Dependant relatives would have to cope. God needed more men.

He was particularly hard on conscientious objectors. The Quakers, those with religious scruples, he had to excuse, but those who objected on political grounds on grounds of personal conscience earned his condemnation.

"God is waging war against evil," he would thunder. "Do you refuse to stand at his side?"

He would gladly have imprisoned them for the duration of the war, or longer, or even had them shot, but the law was far too soft. There were other options: non-combatant roles: stretcher-bearers, medical corps, labour corps behind the lines. There were those who saw even this as being support for the war and refused. Court martial and imprisonment was the fate that awaited them.

Pomfret was particularly pleased when Joe Wainwright appeared before him.

"On what grounds are you claiming exemption?" he enquired mildly.

"I've no quarrel with the ordinary German working man."

"Even though this exemplary German working man is now a soldier raping and shooting Belgian civilians?"

"That's old propaganda."

"You've travelled extensively in France and Belgium have you Mr Wainwright? You have first hand knowledge, denied to the foreign correspondents of our distinguished press."

"Distinguished press!" Joe almost spat. "They print what they're told to print."

"You're remarkably opinionated for a junior clerk at the counting house at Empire Mill," Pomfret purred.

There was a ripple of amusement from the observers.

"I know this much. It's the land owning capitalist class in this country that are my enemies, not the German working man."

"So those set in authority over you are your enemies are they?"

"They're are the ones working men all over the world should unite and fight."

"Well you won't be surprised if your enemy decides you're a dangerous fellow and should be locked up. Take him away officers."

There was much cheering and clapping as the police manhandled Joe out of the room. Pomfret could not suppress a smile. It was his finest moment.

Chapter Thirty

"Hello sleeping beauty's awake, Sam."

Ben was in a trench, reduced by shellfire to little more than a depression out in no man's land. There were three others there.

"Looks like he's had a row with Jack Johnson, Sid."

Only one of Ben's eyes would open. The other was sealed by swollen flesh. He reached up to feel, and encountered his face before he expected to. All that side of his face was swollen and throbbing. There was pain too from his left thigh. He was scared to look, scared what he might see, or not see. He twisted at last to look. The leg was still there, still at a normal angle. The stuff of his khaki trousers was dark with blood, but there was no blood flowing. He could move the leg. He decided the wound was superficial. He noticed a bullet had pierced his box respirator.

The others lying there were also wounded, but much more

seriously. Sam in the chest; Sid in the stomach. The third man who was unconscious had a bad leg wound. He was an officer. He was a lieutenant. He was Lieutenant Nathanial Shaw. Ben's blood began to rush causing his face to throb more painfully. His breathing became more difficult. He realised he still had his rifle in his hand..

"That'd be a blighty one, if he could get back," Sid said, nodding at the lieutenant's smashed leg.

Ben had his rifle ready. If only the others hadn't been there, he could have emptied a clip of ammo into him.

"Go on. We're not likely to say anything," Sam said, seeming to divine his intention.

Ben looked at them more closely. Sam's chest gaped and his ribs were poking out. He could see the back of the trench through the hole in Sid's stomach. Their faces were the colour of rotting bone.

"Leave him. He's not going anywhere with that leg?" Sid advised. "He's going to die anyway. Why have it on your conscience?"

There was the crackle of rifle fire.

"That's Fritz," Sam said, "picking off the wounded. "We'd put a few rounds over to keep their heads down, but... A twitch of his blood encrusted sleeves was as near as he could get to a shrug of helplessness.

Ben turned and elbowed himself to the edge of the trench. Two hundred yards away a number of Germans were standing on the parapet aiming at the wounded out in no man's land.

He eased his rifle into position. Fortunately his right cheek was sound and it nestled against the stock. He squeezed the trigger, worked the bolt, squeezed the trigger, worked the bolt, squeezed the trigger, worked the bolt. Three of the Germans fell back into the trench, the others jumped.

"Now if they can work out where we are, we'll have a few shells over in a minute," Sid said, "Not that it matters to us."

They waited. There was no response.

"What time is it?" Ben asked.

"Time? I don't even know what day it is." Sam said.

Ben looked up at the sky. The rain had stopped, but it was still grey.

"When it gets dark, we'll try and get back."

"You can," Sid said. "We're not going anywhere, nor is his Nibs, unless you carry him."

Ben had neither eaten nor drunk for over 36 hours, but he wanted nothing. He felt sick. His head felt huge. The swelling extended so far, it distorted his lips. It throbbed painfully. There was a gash at the back of his left hand where a bullet had grazed him. His whole hand was red with dried blood. He'd had some near misses, but was still alive. Had he been spared so he could end up in the same trench as Nathanial Shaw? Hadn't fate brought them together so he could avenge her?"

"Plug him Ben," Sam urged. "If it hadn't been for him, you and Sadie could have been getting married after this is all over."

"Don't listen to him, Ben." Sid warned. "Face it Sadie's the bonniest lass in Over Darren and for many miles beyond. Why should she be interested in you? She'd be bound to go for good-looking chaps with summat about 'em like Mick Moon and his Nibs."

"Ben's as good as anybody."

"What, his mother has a pie shop and his father's a drunk!"

"What about her? Lord knows where her father is, and her mother's a cripple."

"That's hardly her fault., and she runs that stall all on her own."

"Not now she doesn't, not now she's got her little bastard to look after."

"That's not her fault either."

"What? Wasn't she there when it happened?"

" Of course she's partly to blame, but just think; he turns up with his posh ways, plenty of money and his racing car. You know what lasses are like."

The argument went back and forth in Ben's head. The argument that had gone back and forth in his head for weeks. He realised then that Sam and Sid were not real. He knew he must be delirious. The two men lying there had been dead for days. Was Nathanial dead too? Ben edged nearer for a better look. Was his chest rising and falling? His face was white with loss of blood.

He stared into the immobile, darkly shadowed features. He stared at those bloodless lips that had kissed Sadie's. He brought his rifle up and aimed it at the heart, the heart that had raced with passion when Sadie had been in his embrace. He squeezed the trigger.

Nathanial Shaw's eyes opened; innocent blue eyes. Ben stood his rifle down.

Shaw's pain-haunted eyes opened and widened at the sight of Ben's battered and bloody face.

"Who are you?" he whispered.

Ben's training conditioned his response.

"Private Preston, D Company, sir."

Shaw's white face twisted with pain and the blue shadows there shifted and elongated.

"Where are we?"

"About 200 yards from Fritz, sir."

Ben knew it was going to be harder to shoot him now, now that he was conscious, now that they had communicated.

"I know you, don't I?" Shaw asked.

"I worked in the counting house at Empire Mill, sir."

Shaw nodded. Ben decided to goad him.

"I'm a friend of Sadie O'Donnell's, sir"

Shaw's eyes widened and for a few seconds he forgot the pain, but he said nothing and closed his eyes again.

"It's a boy, sir You've got a son."

Ben held his rifle at the ready.

"You're damned insolent, Private."

Ben was determined to goad him further.

"She's called him Ewart, sir. He's doing well. They both are."

"I don't know what the Devil it's got to do with you Preston, but I know I should have done more for her."

"Paid her off, sir."

Shaw shook his head.

"No, married her. If I get out of this hole, I will do. I will marry her."

Ben's grip on his rifle slackened. He sat back.

"Marry her," he whispered.

Shaw nodded.

"Yes I'll go up to Cara and ask her to marry me."

"She's not there. Pomfret's booted them off."

"What right has he…"

In his agitation he'd jarred his leg and the pain overcame him.

Ben saw Sadie married to Nathanial Shaw, living somewhere like Woodlands. The boy would have the best of everything, the best education. Didn't she deserve such a life? Wouldn't she be happy? What could he give her – a back to back in the shadow of the mill, barely enough to live on and only the Church School and the Mill in prospect for the boy. If Sadie married Shaw, he would one day own Empire Mill.

"Do you mean it? Would you marry her?"

"I'd marry her, if I only got the chance."

"I'll get you out. I'll carry you out when it gets dark."

"You! I'm a head taller than you Preston."

"I'm stronger than I look. I'll carry you out, but for her sake, not for yours.

Chapter Thirty One

"Anybody who isn't in church on Sunday, needn't come into work on Monday morning, because they'll be fired."

Pomfret sat back and let the import of his words sink in with his fellow board members.

Eddie Moy ran his hand over his face. He could feel his ulcer tuning up. Empire Mill was a sinking ship and there was nobody on the bridge who had a clue what to do. All Evelyn had been bothered about was making sure the crew were comfortable, now here was this one steering them towards the rocks. If Peregrine had been coming back, he'd have hung on, tried to keep the business afloat. Now he thought he'd be better off jumping ship. He said nothing.

Cyril Ellison cleared his throat.

"I've no quarrel with your sentiments Reverend, but it's hard enough to keep workers as it is, we can't compete with the wages in munitions."

"The war against evil is not just being waged in France and Flanders, it's being fought here in Over Darren," Pomfret intoned. "I have it on good authority that men, and women too can you believe, often resort to public houses on a Sunday?"

"They're hardly open now with these new licensing restrictions," Cyril pointed out.

"They shouldn't be open at all."

There was the ghost of a smile flitting about Old Hindle's lips as he spoke.

"It might be a difficult one to enforce, Pomfret. They're not all in your flock. If Jack says he was at the Particular Baptists and Jill says she attended St Peter's in Chains and Johnnie says he was at the Friends Meeting House, you'll have a hard time of it proving otherwise."

"Nevertheless we'll have notices posted and I'll impress on my brother clergy the need to inform me of absences. Any other comments?" Pomfret looked at Evelyn, but although she found the proposal ridiculous and abhorrent, she was keeping her powder dry.

"Very well next item. I'm very concerned at the number of men of military age that are still employed at the mill. I propose we give them the option of enlisting now, with the promise of their jobs back after the war, or face dismissal."

"These are skilled men you're talking about," Eddie Moy said, "men with years of experience. You can't replace time-served mechanics with young lasses."

"Need I remind you Mr Moy that the men out in France are struggling to hold back the evil Hun at risk of life and limb, while fit, hulking fellows here lie in soft beds every night. If every man of military age did his duty and went to France, the war would be over in weeks."

"So what happens when looms stop?" Eddie asked.

"There are plenty of old men in the workhouse who've spent their lives in mills. We'll use them."

"Taking looms to bits isn't a job for old men. Do you know how

much the engine jacks alone weigh on a box loom?"
Pomfret dismissed the objection with a curl of his lip.
"I'll have a list of men drawn up and issue notices forthwith. Now the next item has been proposed by Miss Shaw," he gave her an indulgent smile. "Perhaps I can ask her to elucidate."
Evelyn had been preparing for this, rehearsing her words. She knew they were all against it and that Pomfret in particular would scorn it. She knew she couldn't win, but she wasn't going down without a fight.
"My proposal is for a convalescent home for our workers to be opened on the island of Cara. As you know my father bought the island shortly before his death. We visited it and found the climate benign and healthy."
"I know the west coast of Scotland," Old Hindle said. "Rain, incessant rain, dreadful place."
"Not on Cara, rainfall figures are lower than for the mainland and snow is almost unknown."
"You've done your homework," Pomfret observed.
Evelyn hesitated, waiting for the sneer, but it never came. She went on:
"Achaglass House on the island is a substantial villa and could be made to serve with very little alteration. The gardens are very well laid out and with the addition of shelters and benches would be perfect for gentle exercise. "
"We've discussed this before Miss Shaw," Eddie said. "I'm not against it in principle, but we can't afford it. You would need nurses; you would need a doctor; you would need servants, cooks, gardeners. I vote we shelve it, look at it again after the war when times improve."
"The health of some of our workers is very poor," Evelyn said. "Over Darren has the highest rates of pulmonary illness in the country. Part of this is due to climate, but much of it to inhaling cotton fibres. We have a duty to these people. Our infant mortality rate is twice what it is in some towns."
"Maybe if we deducted a sum from earnings and built up a fund,"

Cyril said.

"They earn little enough as it is," Evelyn snapped.

Pomfret raised a big hand. 'This is it', thought Evelyn, and prepared to fight her corner.

"I approve of the idea. Naturally I would want to see some provision for the spiritual welfare of our workers in place, a task I'm happy to undertake, but I propose we ask Miss Shaw to come up with some costs and we'll implement the scheme forthwith."

Evelyn stared at him. Eddie Moy passed his hand over his face.

"Put my name down. I could do with a month there," he groaned.

The meeting was brought to a close.

"How is he?" Sadie asked. She and Becky were back at the mill. They came in together at the end of the day. Rose mimed breathing difficulties and Sadie flew upstairs. The room was full of smoke.

"What's the matter with this fire?" Becky asked. Rose threw her hands up and mimicked the swirling smoke. It was a wild, wet day and by dint of puffing out her cheeks and fluttering her fingers conveyed that the fire always smoked when it was wet and windy. Becky wafted a clear space in the smoke. Sadie was back.

"He's got a fever and he's struggling to breathe. He needs a doctor." Ewart had fallen ill shortly after their return, intensifying their gloom.

"The doctor won't come unless he knows he's going to be paid." Becky said.

"He'll be paid when we are," Sadie.

Becky put her shawl back on.

"I'm going to see his Grandma. We'll have a good doctor to him, if I have to shake her till her teeth fall out."

She turned out again and battled against the wind and rain. The reflections from the street corner gas lamps were scribbled on the wet flags. There were not many folk about on such a wild night. She had Perseverance Lane to herself. She was wet through by the time she arrived at the front door. It was dry in the porch. She pulled on the bell and was all ready to hammer on the door by the time Barltrop arrived. She didn't waste any words on him and left him floundering. She knew her way and marched through to the drawing room.

Pomfret, Esther and Evelyn were there and Becky had the impression high words were being exchanged. Becky confronted Esther seated by a roaring fire, black ribbons still in her snowy hair.

"Your grandson's ill. He needs a doctor."

"What's the meaning of this?" Pomfret demanded.

Esther drew herself up, her arms folded under her considerable bosom.

"I have no grandchild."

Evelyn intervened and took Becky by the shoulders.

"It's alright. I'll phone for Dr Howard, and get Dickens to drive us back."

In the car Becky explained.

"He fell ill as soon as we got back and is it any wonder? You don't realise how filthy this place is until you've got away. The air's not fit to breathe."

"I put our idea for a convalescent home on Cara to the Board and Pomfret agreed to it."

"What!"

"That was my reaction, but I found out the catch tonight. Ephraim Neville, Pomfret's accomplice has asked him for my hand in marriage. It seems all will be sweetness and light if I say yes, otherwise Cara will be cleared and deer introduced for shooting parties."

"What are you going to do?"

"Mother says I'm lucky to get an offer at my age."

"That's just like Esther. Anyway you don't need a man. No woman does"

"I know. I don't, but think of all those who will benefit if I agree."

Dr Howard attended promptly. He grimaced in distaste at the smoke-filled room and went up the narrow stairs. They could hear the floor boards creak as he moved about above them. The stairs creaked as he descended.

He waved the smoke away irritably.

"This won't do him any good. "

Rose began her pantomime. Dr Howard regarded her with professional interest.

"She's saying the fire doesn't draw in this weather," Becky explained.

"Stroke?"

Becky nodded.

"She could be helped if you got her into hospital."

"And who would pay?"

"What about Ewart?" Sadie wailed.

"Chest's inflamed. He's a strong baby. You've done well. He has a chance. I'll have something made up and sent round. Keep him warm and for goodness sake try and keep this smoke out of his room. I'll call tomorrow." He lifted his hat to Evelyn and was gone. The three women stood in silence, each lost in her own fog of despair.

Chapter Thirty Two

Before it got dark, Ben studied the stretch of no man's land that lay between them and their own front line. It was a muddy moonscape, a desolation of broken ground, hostile to life, littered with splintered posts; smashed duck boards; rusty barbed wire; discarded equipment; flashes of foul water, and over all lay a patina distilled from mud, blood and smoke. How to find a way back through that in the dark and carrying a wounded man.

There were three shattered tree stumps leaning awry, the end one was the tallest and had some vestigial branches. He remembered seeing them ahead of him, when he came over the top. If he could get there, he should be able to recognise the profile of Hill 60 and their own front line.

There was a baulk of timber in the trench that had once formed the parapet of a dugout. Ben hefted it into position so that it pointed towards the three trees. If it was too dark to see them, then at least they could set off in the right direction. A moonlit night might make it easier for the Germans to spot them, but it would make it so much easier to find a way back.

Sometimes Nathanial was unconscious. Sometimes his eyes were open. What were his chances? The leg was smashed. If gangrene took hold, he'd lose it. If he didn't get attention soon, he would die. Wouldn't it be kinder just to put a bullet through his head? Ben wasn't sure he could do that now. Just leave him then, get back himself and alert a rescue party. No, he was doing this for Sadie, doing it so she could have a better life than he could give her, doing it so when she was living the life of a lady, he'd know it was he who'd given it to her.

He dozed himself and when he awoke it was so dark, he couldn't see across the trench to where Nathanial lay. There was no moon. There were no stars. The cloud persisted. This was impossible. He waited until his eyes could detect differences in the density of the shadow, could begin to discern shapes. He could see where the top of the trench ended and the sky began now. He could see a thickening of the shadow that might be Nathanial's body. He crawled towards it.

He reached out and his fingers encountered the officer's tunic. Had Sadie's fingers once toyed with those buttons?

"Are you awake, sir? It's time." He crouched down beside him, wincing from the wound in his thigh. "Put your arm round my shoulder."

Nathanial stirred reluctantly. Ben groped for his other hand and brought them together round his neck.

"Hold tight and try and push yourself up with your good leg."

Nathanial gasped as new waves of pain overwhelmed him. His efforts were feeble and Ben had to drag him on to his back. Nathanial cried out. There were still cries and moans coming from the wounded in no man's land. Ben froze. There was no response from the German line.

Ben began to crawl forward. He had to pull Nathanial's clenched hands away from his wind-pipe, so that he could breathe. Had he once clasped Sadie with such fervour? He crawled out over the back of the trench, feeling his way along the length of timber. It was too dark to see the three trees. Nathanial's sobbing breath was hot in his ear. So it must have sobbed once in passion in Sadie's ear. Even had he been able to, Ben would have made no effort to lessen Nathanial's pain. He deserved to suffer.

Ben progressed doggedly. He stumbled and was often on all fours, his hands slipping in the mud and impaled on barbed wire. He could still see nothing of the three trees. Suddenly everything was bright, as though a light switch had been thrown. A star-shell had burst and was descending.

Ben froze, but scanned the horizon avidly. There they were, the trees, over to the right. No man's land seemed briefly to be not so endless. He turned his head in the right direction and when all was dark again, began to move on into the blackness, a blackness that, it seemed, might go on for ever.

The ghosts of the three trees went before him. He could still see them when he closed his eyes. Nathanial sometimes gasped, sometimes whimpered, sometimes swore, sometimes gritted his teeth, sometimes muttered a prayer, but he hung on. He clung on, even when Ben stumbled, even when Ben slithered in the mud. He hung on. He clung on. He knew Ben was his only hope and he wasn't going to let go.

By now the after-image of the trees had faded. Ben was just keeping going, just avoiding the water-filled craters and the thickets of barbed wire, though sometimes he was snagged and precious reserves of his strength were lost tearing himself free. His only plan was to keep going until he collapsed, wait for daylight and see where they were then.

And then it was daylight, briefly. Another star-shell burst. Ben froze again and again peered avidly. No sign of the trees. Before the light died, he glanced behind. They were there. The trees were behind them. Had they passed them, or had they gone in a circle and were they now crawling back towards the German line?

Ben waited in the dark. His lungs were labouring. His heart was hammering. His legs trembled with fatigue. His arms trembled with fatigue. What should he do? Which way should he go? Should he turn round and head the other way? He knew his strength was ebbing. Should he put Nathanial down and rest? He waited in the dark, panting, not knowing what to do.

Then there was machine gun fire, a burst of manic jabbering that he knew at once was German. It came from behind. They'd got beyond the trees. The front line must be only a short distance away.

Encouraged, Ben forged ahead.

"Not far, sir," he gasped.

There was no answer, but Nathanial hung on. He was still breathing.

They reached the British wire.

"I'll have to set you down, while I find the gap."

Ben crouched down, but Nathanial would not let go. Ben forced his hand apart and dumped him. Nathanial cried out.

It was a cry that rang out all over no man's land. Ben crouched, not moving, waiting for the wire to ignite with blue sparks as the machine gun bullets played up and down it. Nothing, no there was something: noise and stealthy movement not far away – a raiding party. Please God let it be one of ours.

"Who goes there?" hissed the challenge.

"It's me," Ben whispered.

"It's me! What kind of answer is that? What's the password? Quick or I'll blow your head off."

Ben knew the voice – Major Mustard.

"I've just come in, sir. I've got a wounded man, an officer."

That, as he knew it would, made a difference.

"Where is he? Who is it?" Ben told him. "Right, leave it to me."

"Is that you, Ben?" Yorky's voice.

It was Yorky who led him through the wire and back into their line.

Later in the reserve trench Ben drank hot tea and was as comfortable leaning back against corrugated iron as if he'd been on silken cushions.

"Dougie's gone west. Smithie's not back," Yorky said.

"He won't be," Ben said and the image of the flaming skull rushed at him again.

"So you brought Romeo in. I though you were going to plug him."

"Not for his sake, for hers. He says he'll marry her."

"Well if he does do, I'll show my backside on the Town Hall steps."

Pat passed by. The last two days had added years to him. A muddy, blood-stained bandage was wrapped round his hand. He stopped to look at Ben, examining his bruised face.

"You're not going to win a beauty contest."

"He's got it all worked out this one," Yorky said, indicating Ben. "He carries Romeo in on his back, knowing if Fritz lets fly it'll be Romeo who gets it up the backside."

"Did Ben bring him in? They're saying Major Mustard brought him in. They're saying he'll get a gong for it, maybe a VC."

Yorky flared up

"That's not right! That's not right. It were Ben brought him in. I'm going to say summat."

Pat held him back.

"Leave it Yorky. You'll only get yourself on the crime sheet."

"It's not right. If anybody's getting a medal it should be Ben. It's the second time..."

"I'm not bothered about medals," Ben said.

"He'll put 'em right anyway," said Pat. "Romeo'll tell 'em it were Ben."

"Do you think so?" said Yorky. "I don't. Officers don't want to be beholden to privates."

"He might not live anyway," Ben said. "His leg's badly smashed up."

"Let's look on the bright side then," said Yorky. "Let's hope he dies."

Chapter Thirty Three

Had Neville showed a hint of smugness, a vestige of arrogance, Evelyn would have shown him the door. In that she was like her father. Jack'd have knocked the swagger out of someone without hesitation, but if they showed any diffidence, any vulnerability, then his sympathetic side came to the fore, albeit larded with pawky humour.

Neville was nervous. The interview clearly meant a lot to him and cost him an effort. Evelyn noted this new aspect of him, but was too indignant at the pressure Pomfret had applied on his behalf to soften her demeanour. She maintained an upright posture, hands clasped and resting in her lap and said not a word to ease his plight.

Neville leaned forward in his chair. He was wringing his hands.

"Miss Shaw, I felt it only proper to seek Charles's approval before approaching you, and he was kind enough to pledge his recommendation."

"His recommendation carries no weight with me."

"But you'll own his motives are generous."

Evelyn's anger kindled.

"All I see is that he makes his support of my plans to alleviate the plight of our workers conditional on my accepting your proposal of marriage."

"He went too far," Neville admitted unhappily.

"Indeed he did."

"But he means well."

Evelyn stared at him.

"Is it possible you don't see through him? His only interest in seeing you married to me is to extend his influence over my family."

It was Neville's turn to stare.

"Well he misjudges me. If I had the happiness to become dear to you, then my loyalty would be to you, not to him. I would be your ally, not his. You don't know for how many years I have admired and esteemed you How the hope of winning your affection has been always before me, informing everything I have done, inspiring my every endeavour. You've been dear to me Miss Shaw ever since I was the most junior assistant at the library, and at every promotion, until I was fortunate enough to be made Chief Librarian I have rejoiced because I thought it made me worthier of you. I can truly say with my hand on my heart, Miss Shaw, that I have loved you ever since I was first capable of harbouring such an emotion."

His eloquence went a long way towards convincing himself and some way towards convincing Evelyn. It was the only time a man had made a protestation of love to her. She'd schooled herself to believe that it would never happen. She was not unmoved.

"I was not aware of the strength of your feelings …"

"I love you Miss Shaw," Neville was stirred by the sound of his proclamation. "I love you Miss Shaw."

"Mr Neville, I need time to consider my response."

"Take it, Miss Shaw. Just so long as you don't blight all my hopes, take all the time you want. I will wait. I am content to wait, and hope."

He rose seemingly anxious to leave before she should rethink and give the negative answer he'd feared.

For some time Evelyn remained seated, and now it was she who was wringing her hands.

The days approaching the winter solstice in Over Darren were usually chilly, damp and foggy. Unusually this year a hard frost took hold. The grass on the mill fields was white. The surface of the mill lodge froze and grew dull. Soot black traceries of twigs were transformed into frosted fronds. The moors over the town turned white.

Healthy folk, vigorous folk walked briskly with glowing cheeks and smoking breath. The old and the sick turned blue and crept along, hunched against the bitter weather.

As the 21st day approached vital forces ebbed. The hours grew dim. A dark eternity loomed. Many were touched by gloomy apprehensions, crossed in endeavours, small and large, thwarted in their hopes. For many the darkness gathered round menacingly.

Paradoxically the still, cold weather cured the smoking chimney and the fire burned brightly and clearly in Ewart's sick room. The child was restless, his breathing was passionate, his colour hectic. Dr Howard called, declared him a 'battler' and left shaking his head.

Sadie and her mother were sitting by the bed, their shadows flung up by fire-light like monstrous malefactors. Becky came in bringing a blast of cold air.

"How is he?" She looked down at him.

"The same," Sadie said.

"Will he take anything?"

"Just boiled water."

Becky went over to warm her hands. Her fingers tingled.

"Nathanial Shaw's been wounded."

Sadie looked round, her eyes big with alarm.

"He's alright, leg wound. He's back in England at Queen Mary's Military Hospital."

Sadie said nothing. Her face was immobile. Her thoughts raced.

"Perhaps you should go and see him," Becky said.

"Not I! Let her go - his fiancée."

"He should be told about Ewart."

"Do you think he'd be interested.?"

"I don't know, but he's the lad's father."

"We don't need his help."

"Ewart does. He could be in hospital, have proper nursing."

Sadie's eyes grew dark. Her thoughts were in turmoil. She'd just been concentrating on Ewart, willing him to get better. Now this, and she didn't know what to think. The hopes Nathan had stirred in her during those long ago days of motoring in the countryside and the long nights of love in faraway hotels had long been buried. Could they be resurrected?

"Do what you want."

"I'll speak to Evelyn," Becky said and sought to divine the future in the burning coals.

They were in the morning room after breakfast. The only sound was the solemn ticking of the clock on the mantelpiece and the rustle of Pomfret's paper. Esther was drafting menus for the Christmas 'at home'; Evelyn making calculations for equipping the convalescent home.

"Jane will have to go, Charles," Esther said. "She can't cook. It's a wonder you've survived all these years."

Despite his girth and stature, Pomfret was not over concerned about his food. The stodgy puddings and soggy pastries Jane had served up had been quite acceptable to him.

"She can't control those two silly girls. I caught Ann in the pantry with the butcher's boy the other day. I can't be watching them all the time. I know it wouldn't be right before Christmas, but I'll give her her notice in the New Year."

Pomfret folded his paper at a new page with a gesture of irritation. He preferred to have Jane under his eye. He wondered if he could fob her off on Neville. If he managed to land Evelyn, they'd need a housekeeper.

Barltrop appeared and journeyed across the room towards Esther, silver tray quaking in his hand.

"Telegram for Mrs Pomfret."

Esther's face turned as white as her hair. Her hand made meaningless fumblings at her throat.

"No," she gasped. "No, not Nathan."

For a moment they formed a tableau: Esther slumped back, Evelyn leaning forward, Pomfret with his paper lowered.

Evelyn moved first, her heart racing. She took the telegram. There was another envelope on the tray. Pomfret had folded his paper, his mind full of implications.

Evelyn read. Only the word 'wounded' leapt out at her.

"Oh mother, it's alright. He's only wounded. And there's a letter from him."

Esther was breathing with difficulty, her mouth agape. Evelyn's words seemed to have made no impact.

"He's here," Evelyn read. "He's here at Queen Mary's."

She ran to her mother and knelt by her.

"He's home mother. He's safe."

Esther burst into tears.

"I can't stand this," she sobbed. "Oh how can anybody stand this?"

"He's safe mother."

"No," she sobbed. "They'll make him better and send him back. How do they think mothers can stand this?"

"They won't send him back. They won't." And now Evelyn was crying too. "They won't send him back. He's lost the leg."

The two women clung to each other and wept. Pomfret patted Esther's shoulder abstractedly and wondered how this would affect his plans.

Chapter Thirty Four

Dawn brought no thaw and little light. With its white roof tops, Over Darren was a tented town, a town of black and white. Its black steeples and towers were edged with white, its tall chimneys so many undotted i's and uncrossed t's on a white background.

Old folk picked their way carefully; youngsters careered full tilt through the snow hammering it into bottle glass with their clogs. The trams kept running, the clamour of their iron wheels muffled by the snow. On the moors above the town the sheep looked quite black against the snow. On the fells of Hoddersdale the grouse shooting had ended and quite satisfactory totals were entered in the game book.

There was snow in France and Flanders too. Around Ypres the mud had turned to iron. The surface water had frozen. Corpses were frosted over. Shells landing on this hard ground flung shrapnel far and wide. A man could be killed by a shell exploding hundreds of yards away.

The wind blew from the east, from icy wastes that never thawed, from lands of unimaginable cold, where breath froze and exposed flesh turned white and brittle. It blew from white lands inimical to man, inimical to all life of flesh and blood.

The wind was at the Germans' backs. They could turn up the collars of their great coats and hunch their shoulders against it. The wind was in the faces of the Allies, in their eyes, making them water when they tried to look out over no man's land.

They donned all the clothing they had, sheepskins over their great coats, gloves, scarves, balaclavas sent from home, but still they were cold, still they blew on frozen fingers, stamped frozen feet, hugged freezing bodies with freezing arms.

Hot tea was bliss, even tainted with petrol from the tins they brought the water up in. Hot stew was a blessing too, even if it was only bully beef and tinned vegetables. The rum ration was a life saver, but not for Ben. He gave his to Yorky.

"That's another plate of egg and chips I owe you," he said, pouring it carefully into his spare water bottle. "You won't have to put your hand in your pocket next time we're in Pops."

They'd just been stood down after the dawn watch. Somebody somewhere was frying bacon.

"Just smell that," Yorky said. "What I wouldn't give for half a dozen rashers, eggs, sausages, fried tomatoes and a pint mug of strong sweet tea. If we ever get out of this Ben, I'll make you the best breakfast you've ever had in your life…"

Suddenly there was uproar. Empty shell cases suspended all along the front line were ringing, being banged with shovels, bayonets, rifles buts and fists.

"Gas! Gas! Gas!"

They looked out over the parapet and saw it: a grey/green cloud like a bank of moorland mist, the colour of a long dead German. It rolled in towards them, tendrils smoked, snaked in advance of the body of it, feeling a way over the frozen, broken ground. It came slowly, but inexorably, propelled by the malevolent east wind.

Men were momentarily mesmerised, but then; pandemonium, as they got out gas masks, pulled them on, fixed bayonets, got bombs ready. The gas was only the first wave, behind would be waves of Germans.

The material of Ben's gas helmet abraded the raw flesh of his bruised face. He tucked the ends of it into the collar of his great coat, wishing he'd sewn the top button back on. He was at once in another world. The frantic activity all around him seemed suddenly far away, remote, beyond the sound of his own breathing. His vision was distorted. The men around him had become freak-show characters, grotesques.

The gas hesitated at the parapet of the trench, then tumbled in, filling it up and pouring out on the far side. To Ben it was a moorland mist, one such as he'd been lost in once, lost on moors that he knew like the streets around his own home, lost and near to panic, until he recognised the outline of the Jubilee Tower looming above him.

There were monsters emerging from the mist now, a long line of them advancing, monsters with the bodies of men and the heads of monstrous flies, bulbous eyed with swaying proboscises, monsters with rifles, rifles with bayonets fixed.

Ben's rifle felt unfamiliar to him. His hands could make no sense of it. His fingers were too thick and clumsy to find the trigger. When he looked down at it, the parapet seemed to be falling away from him. He couldn't breathe. The fight for breath dominated all. He couldn't move. He was paralysed. If he could just move his hand, or foot. If he could just move a finger. If he could move, he would be able to breathe again. He was in a dream he'd had many times, a dream of being buried alive, a dream of being suffocated, a dream that persisted even after awakening. A voice from within told him not to struggle, to give in, to let the darkness overwhelm him.

The parapet of the trench flew up again, flew past him, soared away far above him, and he was gone.

It was the surgeon at the Advanced Dressing Station who had sawed off the leg. Nathanial had been lying out in no man's land too long and the stench of gangrene was already evident. The surgeon was a Scot with protuberant, pale blue eyes. He said.

"You won't think so yet, but you're lucky. Losing that leg has probably saved you your life. You're out of it now. 2nd lieutenants don't live long in the front line."

Nathanial didn't feel lucky. He was embittered. He was a cripple, a creature to be pitied. No more horse riding; no more motoring. Marrying Sadie was all he was fit for now. He stared at the flat cover on the bed, where his leg should be, a leg he could still feel.

It was a bloody and harrowing business, the journey in the ambulance back to the Casualty Clearing Station at HQ. From there he was sent by train to Boulogne and thence to Southampton.

Queen Mary's Hospital near Over Darren had been built as an asylum, but its completion had coincided with the outbreak of war, and it had been requisitioned for use as a military hospital. A siding linked it to the main line and men disembarked from the boat at Southampton could be taken by train straight to the hospital.

Esther and Evelyn were his first visitors. They found him restless and peevish and thin. Evelyn had meant to open the subject of Sadie and Ewart. The child had survived the crisis point, but Dr Howard pronounced him fatally weakened and predicted he wouldn't survive Over Darren's unhealthy climate. She wanted to secure his agreement to send him and his family back to Cara, but she knew this was not the time to ask.

Nathan was more gracious with his next visitor, Caroline. She swept through the ward in her long black winter coat with its fur collar. She had a gracious smile for everyone. It was warm on the ward. She unbuttoned her coat and fanned her face with her gloves. She seemed so vigorous and vital and full of life. He felt a paltry thing beside her.

"Oh Nathan I'm so sorry." She glanced at the flat expanse on the bed.

He nodded, too full of emotion to speak.

"The thing is you're alive and you're going to stay alive."

"A poor specimen though."

"Don't say that. You're still you." She lay down her gloves and took his hands in hers. "You don't think this makes any difference do you? You don't think I feel any differently about you, or if I do it's to think more highly of you, knowing what you've endured, what you've suffered."

"But I'll never ride a horse again, or drive a car. I'd not be much use at the Boxing Day meet."

"Oh what does that matter? There's so much more for us. Think of all the work that will need doing, if we move into Carstairs. It's a lovely old house, but it needs practically rebuilding. And you can take up carriage driving and we will have a chauffeur. And now we can plan our wedding. We don't have to wait until this dreadful war is over."

Caroline had resurrected his dreams, his dreams of the life he'd hoped to lead, the life of a country gentleman, on equal terms with the best in society, entertaining the cream of the county in his country home and visiting them in their homes. What kind of life would he have with Sadie? How could he introduce her to the county set? And yet he had made a vow. He felt uneasy.

"In view of what's happened Caroline, I'm freeing you from your promise."

She squeezed his hands and leaned forward so that her honest, handsome face was only inches from his.

"I don't want to be freed and I'm not going to free you. Just you try and there'll be a breach of promise case."

Here was Nathan's moment, his opportunity to tell her about Sadie and see if she still didn't want to be freed. He didn't do so.

"Daddy's so proud of you. It was a fellow officer went out to bring you in wasn't it?"

Another opportunity for Nathan to redeem himself, to tell the truth, but he was beginning to see his life in a new light, beginning to see a new destiny for himself. Didn't he deserve something after all he'd suffered? Wasn't it right that he should readjust past events?

"Yes, Major Forrester, a splendid chap."

"He deserves a kiss from me for saving you."

"If there are any kisses going spare…"

They laughed, rubbed noses and stared into each others eyes.

It was in the hospital at Boulogne where Ben finally resurfaced. There had been wretched periods of consciousness earlier, when his lungs and stomach had been trying to turn themselves inside out. Long periods when every breath had had to be wrenched painfully from the air. There'd been long periods of delirium, long periods where he'd struggled to keep his head above the surface of bilious waves, periods when he shrank from monstrous flies, periods when anxious faces loomed and doleful voices tolled at his bedside. But it was in the hospital at Boulogne when he at last recovered something like a normal awareness of the world.

There'd been a bullet hole in his gas helmet, one of the near misses he'd had going over the top at Hill 60. He'd lain at the bottom of the trench where the gas was at its thickest for some time until the German attack had been fought off and his comrades could carry him out.

His chances had not been assessed as good and he'd been laid to one side at the Advanced Dressing Station while they attended to more promising cases. He'd been found to be breathing when they at last got round to him, so he'd been sent to the Casualty Clearing Station and then Boulogne.

A big, blonde Cockney was sitting on the next bed.

"You've got the best Christmas present you'll ever get mate."

Ben tried to speak.

"It's alright mate. I know you can't say nothing."

A nurse was passing.

"Tell him Morag."

"I'm not called Morag."

"All Scots girls are called Morag."

"Aye, just as all soldiers are called Tommy."

"You can call me Tommy. I don't mind, but tell my mate the good news."

She turned to Ben. She was a rather prim, thin-faced, well-spoken lady.

"The doctor thinks your lungs have to be given a chance to recover, to get plenty fresh air in them."

"He's one of them Lancashires, Morag. There's no fresh air up there. It's all mill chimneys."

"Aye it's a pity he can't get some good Highland air into his lungs."

"You still haven't told him, Morag."

She sighed and turned back to Ben.

"You're going home Ben."

"There you are mate. I told you – the best Christmas present you'll ever get."

Ben closed his eyes. He couldn't believe it. He was going home.

Chapter Thirty Five

The dull winter fields of Hampshire rattled by. There was no war here, no front line up ahead, no whiz bangs to fear, no gas, no need to keep your head down. The farm labourers walking up the lane had nothing to fear. What was the war to them? They might talk about the latest news of it in the tap room at the end of the day. They might have loud opinions about what should be done, but they knew nothing about it.

Their fields were peaceful and undisturbed. Their barns and cottages and villages were intact. No bodies lay rotting in the open. There were no shallow graves of the dead, waiting to be disinterred and dismembered by the next incoming shell. There was no barbed wire, no network of trenches, no Germans dug in on the crests of the rolling downs aiming murderous machine gun fire. Ben had only been back in England a few hours, but felt alienated.

There were more unmistakable echoes of war in the towns they passed through. There were soldiers on the platforms; soldiers going on leave; soldiers coming back from leave; wounded soldiers; soldiers with missing limbs; soldiers on crutches; soldiers in wheelchairs; soldiers on stretchers. It seemed to Ben that the civilians who passed by did so with averted eyes and gave them wide berths. He knew his own battered face, muddied and bloodied great coat caused people to turn away, to avoid looking at him.

He felt apprehensive approaching Over Darren. Would Nathanial have proposed to Sadie? Should he go and see her, or keep out of the way? What would his mother have to say about it? He didn't want to have to listen to her giving Sadie a bad name. Should he own up to the part he'd played? Maybe she knew already, if Nathanial had made an announcement.

It seemed as though a century had passed since he'd last been on Over Darren Station, en route for training camp. It was late afternoon and there were not many travellers; one or two elderly ladies with porters in tow, wheeling their luggage, porters who were often older than they were. His mother would still be in the shop. He'd written, but had been shipped home so quickly, he doubted she'd have got the letter.

He was glad of the gloom of the gas-lit streets, glad there was little chance he'd be recognised, little chance anyone would notice a ghost from the past flitting by. The window of Sally-Anne's shop was aglow. She was busy getting ready for the rush when the mills finished. Unaware she was being observed, her face was grim, the lines of her mouth down-turned. Her features no longer seemed well-defined. Her body had lost shape. She looked old

Ben ducked and strode over the worn step into the steamy shop.

"Won't be a minute love," she said, her back turned as she checked the pies in the oven. She turned.

"What will it be...?"

The shock on her face shocked Ben. She'd gone as white as her pinafore, her hands clutched at her throat. It was as if she feared he was a ghost.

"Ben! Is it you?"

She came out from behind the counter. She wanted to touch him, embrace him, but all the old awkwardness was there. The barrier fell between them. She reached out, and so did he. They clasped hands. They shook hands. They were more like acquaintances than mother and son.

"Your face!" she exclaimed.

Smithy's skull flew out of the darkness at him. His voice had still not recovered.

"It's alright," he croaked. "It's alright."

"Your voice!"

"Gas," he wheezed. "I've been gassed."

"Oh Ben," she reproached him. "Have you eaten?"

He shook his head.

"I'm going to have to stay till the mill lasses have been in. Take this back to the house with you."

She put a pie in a dish, ladled steaming peas over it and wrapped it in a cloth.

"Here. Get the fire going when you get back. I'll be home by seven."

How strange to be in his own house again. How strange to be able to strike a match without having to shield the flame from the attention of a Fritz sniper. How strange to be quiet and safe and comfortable.

The fire was burning brightly by the time Sally-Ann got in. She was glad of it on such a raw, damp night. She did the talking, bringing him up to date.

"Did you know Joe Wainwright's in prison?"

He shook his head.

"Best place for him too. Do you know what he said at the tribunal? He said he'd no argument with the Germans and wouldn't fight them."

Ben smiled; just like Sam.

"I don't know what you're laughing at? If everybody was like that we wouldn't win the war."

'If everybody was like that, there wouldn't be a war,' Ben thought, but kept it to himself.

"How's Grandad?"

"Oh he keeps going. I don't know how at his age. Still he might not have much longer to go. They say Empire Mill's going bust. No wonder with him in charge, Holy Joe."

"Pomfret?" Ben queried.

"Who else? He'll be running the town next. It might be different now Nathanial Shaw's back. You'll have heard he lost his leg."

Ben's heart began to thud. How much did she know? What was she going to come out with next?

"Course with his wedding coming up, he'll have other fish to fry."

So that was it. He'd asked and she'd accepted. What else did he expect? Although he was staring at a bright fire, the prospect seemed cold and black.

"Once he's in with that lot, he might think running a mill's beneath him."

Ben looked up so quickly, pain stabbed through his face.

"How do you mean, that lot?" His voice was raw and ragged.

"The Hoddersdales. They own half the county."

"He's not wedding Sadie then?"

"Why should he do a thing like that? You don't think he'd do right by her. That poor bairn's been at death's door, but he's never been near. I dare say he'd be relieved if it died."

The fire was burning brightly again, but Ben changed the subject before his mother could probe too deeply.

"How's our Maria?"

She pulled a face.

"I only see her when she wants summat."

"How's Dad?"

"The same. You haven't started on the booze I hope."

Ben shook his head.

"Good lad. I just thought with all you've gone through."

"I give my rum ration to my pal and he buys me egg and chips."

"Oh you can get egg and chips can you? That's alright then."

They were silent. There was just the sound of the coals settling. Sally-Ann studied Ben's face.

"What's it like out there, son?"

How could he tell her? How could he make her see the horror? And why should he try? What was the point of upsetting her? It was impossible anyway. There was a gulf between them that could never be bridged.

"Oh it's not so bad, when you get used to it."

Whether she believed him or not, she didn't pursue it.

"Slice some of that bread and toast it. We'll have a bit of supper."

Ben did as he was asked and got down the toasting fork. Sally-Ann put the kettle on the hob.

Chapter Thirty Six

Word that Ben was back got round and his father, Jimmy, turned up on the doorstep.

"Don't let him in," Sally-Anne warned from inside the house.

It was barely mid-day, but Jimmy was already unfocussed and unsteady. His slipshod grin changed with comical speed to a picture of woeful concern, when he saw the state of Ben's face. He pointed a wavering finger.

"You got that scrapping with Jerry?"

Ben saw the flaming skull again, and nodded.

"Did you bif him - out for the count?" He swung his fist and overbalanced himself. He recovered and grinned. "Hand to hand eh? That's the stuff. I'd give 'em what for, if I was there."

"Tell him I'll give him what for, if he doesn't clear off," Sally-Anne shouted.

Jimmy aimed a disrespectful gesture in her direction.

"You're a good lad." He patted Ben on the shoulder. "You're doing your bit. I envy you. I wish I could get out there."

Ben cleared his throat.

"You'll get your chance, Dad. When there's no more of us young'uns left, they'll be calling up men your age."

Expressions of consternation, dismay and bluster succeeded each other across Jimmy's face.

"I'll be there. I'll be there." He drew himself up to his full height, saluted and fell over. Ben helped him up. Taking advantage of their proximity, Jimmy whispered.

"You couldn't lend your old father a bob or two, son?"

"Don't give him owt," Sally-Anne yelled.

Ben slipped him a shilling. Jimmy winked, gave him a thumbs up and staggered away, limping, already rehearsing the bad leg that he hoped would fool the Army doctors.

Ben walked Over Darren's damp streets. How peaceful it was. How enduring and permanent it all seemed. The chimneys, the churches had been there all his life. It seemed they always would, and yet Over Darren, as a town, was not much more than 50 years old. Ypres had been centuries old, and now barely one stone stood on another. He pictured the streets and shops around him reduced to rubble, with fires and smoke and more shells coming in. Could it happen here? Could those old women wrapped up in their shawls on their way to the shops, one day be fleeing from falling bombs?

To postpone the reckoning, he called at his sister's. Maria lived down Cardigan Street in a house identical to Sally-Anne's. Her husband, Bert, had been in the Boer War and was periodically laid low with recurring malaria. He was in bed now.

Maria had the bath in front of the fire and was washing little Davey, who splashed excitedly at the sight of Ben's uniform.

"Ee Ben your face is a mess," Maria said cheerfully.

He didn't take his coat off. He didn't stop.

The tradition in Over Darren, when calling on friends and family and neighbours, was to knock and walk straight in with a cheery or cheeky greeting on your lips. Ben didn't feel that was appropriate when he called on Sadie, so stood on the doorstep until someone answered. It was Becky.

"Ben!" She scrutinised him. "By God, you've got a shiner there. Come in."

The room was lit only by candles and firelight. Sadie's face was half in shadows and half in golden light. She smiled and then looked concerned.

"Oh Ben, your face!"

"It's not as bad as it looks," he said huskily.

"And your voice!"

"I got gassed. They've sent me home to recover. I'm alright."

"Are you? Are you Ben?" Sadie asked searchingly. "It must be awful over there."

"You get used to it."

"Come on Rose," Becky said. "Let's you and me sit with Ewart so these two can have a talk."

Ben took the rocking chair at the other side of the fire.

"How is the lad?"

Sadie stared into the flames.

"Well, he's getting better, but this place won't do for him, all the smoke and the grime. It won't do your lungs any good either. Oh Ben, if you could breathe the air on Cara."

"You liked it there?"

"It's beautiful. You've no idea."

"Can't you go back?"

Sadie shook her head.

"Even when it's raining, it's lovely. There's something about the light."

There was a pause; Sadie seeing again the white beaches, the crystal water; Ben hesitating before broaching the delicate subject.

"Have you seen Nathanial Shaw?" he said at last.

"No."

Ben could sense her defensiveness, but persisted.

"I was with him out in no man's land. We talked about you."

Sadie looked cross.

"What did he have to say?"

"He said he'd marry you, so I brought him back in."

Sadie's eyes were big and angry.

"Does he think I'd have him? Does he think after the way he's treated me, the way he's treated Ewart that I'd even listen to him?"

"I thought you'd have a better life, you and Ewart. I did it for you, not for him."

Sadie stared at him.

"Ben Preston, you're either a fool or a saint. I don't know which."

There was another pause while Sadie examined this news and Ben gathered his wits and his courage.

"Sadie, you know how much I feel about you…"

She sat back and folded her arms, and Ben knew this wasn't the time, but he went doggedly on with it.

"Ever since I was a child, I've been fond of you, hoped that one day… I know I can't give you the life he could, but if…"

Sadie stopped him.

"No Ben. Don't say it. Not now, not while this war's on. Come back safe and sound and talk to me about it then."

"I can hope then?"

"You can always hope." She gave him a roguish smile. "Just keep yourself safe."

"I will. I'll speak to him though. I'll speak to Nathanial Shaw."

"What about?"

"About you and the boy going back to Cara."

"I don't want any favours off him."

"He owes me though. I was all ready to put a bullet through him, until he said he'd marry you."

"You'd have shot him?"

"I would, after what he'd done to you."

Sadie just stared at him.

Words failed her.

Chapter Thirty Seven

The Reverend Charles Pomfret had decided that the time had come to take the Shaws by the scruff of the neck and give them a good shaking, to impose his authority on them once and for all. He was the head of the household now. His plans to neutralise Evelyn had come to nothing. She'd turned Neville down. The convalescent home scheme was therefore dropped. He made no mention of the fact to Evelyn, waiting for her to bring the subject up. So far she'd been too proud to, but he'd noticed her obvious agitation with satisfaction. He was confident Esther would remain neutral

Since he'd come home, Nathanial had alternated between dark moods when he was never far from the drinks cabinet and hope when he contemplated his prospects after marriage. Esther of course was totally absorbed in the wedding, being only put out by not having been invited up to discuss arrangements with Lady

Hoddersdale.

Pomfret felt confident he could steamroller his plans through. He intended to sell Empire Mill, turn Achaglass House into a hotel, stock the island with deer and make it a luxury resort for select members of the aristocracy and the very wealthy. The link about to be forged with the Hoddersdales would put him in contact with just the sort of people he'd always known he was destined to mingle with.

Pomfret picked his moment, the hour after breakfast when they were all in the morning room. He folded his paper and was about to speak, when Barltrop entered and made slowly across the room towards Nathanial.

"A Private Preston to see you, sir."

Nathanial flushed.

"If he's come begging, send him to the kitchen for a meal," Esther said. "Don't be giving him money; it'll only go on drink."

"Yes, mother," he growled. "Show him into the library, Barltrop."

Ben had smartened himself up, but his great coat still showed signs of hard use and near misses. He might just have come down from the front line.

"Bit different to where we last met, sir," Ben said, looking round at the book-lined room, comfortable leather armchairs, and cheerful fire. For a moment the two men saw again the shallow trench amid the wilderness of broken ground and barbed wire.

"Sorry about the leg, sir."

"These things happen," Nathanial said lowering himself into a chair. "Now what's all this about, Preston? I know I said some rash things back there, before you and the Major got me in..."

"It not about Sadie I've come, sir. She says she wouldn't have had you anyway. It's about Ewart, the boy, your boy. Sadie thinks he'd thrive better if they went back to the island. I've come to ask if you could see your way to letting them go back."

Nathanial felt outraged that the fellow dare talk to him in this way, a mere private, an insignificant clerk. His thin hand gripped the arm of the chair. He'd dearly have loved to thrash him, but knew he couldn't, knew how strong the other was, even if he'd had two legs to stand on. Furthermore getting Sadie and the child out of the way on Cara suited him perfectly. He dreaded Caroline finding out. He exercised great control.

"You think a lot of her don't you, Preston?"

Ben nodded.

"Take her to Cara, bring the lad up as your own and I'll see he's not short of anything."

Ben felt a surge of anger, seeing him trying to slip out of his responsibilities, but he too exercised control.

"Don't know about that, sir, but if you can get Sadie and the boy back there, I'd say we were quits."

Nathanial stared at the fire and swallowed his anger.

"I'll see what I can do, Preston."

"Thank you, sir."

He turned to go.

"Just a minute, Preston."

Nathanial took out his pocket book and held a five pound note out.

Ben stared at it.

"Is that all you're worth, sir?"

He turned and left.

Nathanial was not in fact sure he could carry out his promise. He didn't anticipate a sympathetic response from Pomfret and couldn't be sure of his mother's either. When he returned to the morning room, the conflict was in progress.

"What do you think, Nathanial?" Evelyn said. "Our dear step-father proposes selling Empire Mill."

Nathanial received this with equanimity. He'd no intention of being drawn into the running of the mill and his share of the sale proceeds would come in very handy for out of pocket expenses.

"And what about the convalescent home?" Evelyn demanded.

"I've had a change of heart," Pomfret said.

"Because I didn't fall in with your plans and marry one of your cronies."

"Nothing to do with that."

Esther was oblivious to the squabbling, absorbed in embellishing the margins on one of her lists with drawings of bridesmaids. She looked up.

"It would be nice to have Lord and Lady Hoddersdale stay on the island," she said.

"Of course it would, exactly my sentiments," Pomfret chimed.

"What about the child?" Evelyn demanded, pointing the finger at Nathanial. "If it's to thrive, it needs to breathe pure air."

"If you think I'm allowing that sort of person..." Pomfret began.

"Actually I thought it would be a good idea to pack the lot of them off there," Nathanial said.

"Out of the question," Pomfret said. "If his mother can't look after it, there's always the workhouse."

"He's more right to be there than anybody," came a new voice, a soft voice, a whisper of a voice, like the voice of a ghost. Jane had entered and had been standing there unobserved.

"What do you mean by this impudence?" Pomfret demanded.

"Ma'am has seen fit to give me my notice, so I've nothing to lose by saying my piece." She spoke quietly, but everyone hung on her words.

"Many years ago when Charles first made himself comfortable at my table." She noted the look on Esther's face. "Oh yes he was Charles to me long before he was to you. When poor Bill died Charles persuaded me to sell the shops and buy Ashleigh. I was to move in as his housekeeper, and after a decent interval, we were to be married."

"This is preposterous. Leave the house at once!" Pomfret roared.

Esther held up her hand.

"Let her have her say."

Jane inclined her head.

"Of course before the wedding came off, he'd set his sights higher and was making himself comfortable here. He kept putting off our wedding plans, and then when poor Mr Shaw died, I knew it wasn't going to happen and I'd have to be content to be his housekeeper. Well, now I'm not even that, but I can have my say and see right done before I go. Cara belongs to the little lad."

Pomfret was silent, his eyes smouldering like black pits in the white slab of his face.

"Whatever do you mean?" Esther demanded.

Jane took a paper from her sleeve.

"This is an addition to Mr Shaw's will. Charles took it and hid it safe, but not safe from me. I've kept it by me so that when the time came I could do the right thing. It was written the day Mr Shaw died. You can see he left the island and an allowance to the lad. Charles stole it. I really think he'd stop at nothing short of murder to get his own way, and maybe not even stop at that."

"What!" Pomfret roared. "You dare say that to me, a man of the cloth?"

"That's just it." Jane hissed. "You think the cloth gives you the right. I've watched you. I've studied you. Nobody knows you better than me. I know the darkness in your heart."

"That's enough. Your mistress has dismissed you. As you refuse to leave, I'll summon the police."

Esther had been reading the document carefully, her lips moving. The moment Pomfret feared had arrived: Esther was showing her steel.

"Be quiet Charles. It is as she says and here's your name. You did witness it!"

"I tried to talk him out of it, but you know how stubborn he was."

"And you didn't burn it!"

"I was shocked. I wasn't thinking straight. All I wanted was to protect you from those scheming women, from that Jezebel who tempted your son. Besides it means nothing. It's not valid in law. We can still arrange matters as we wish."

"We?" Esther said quietly.

"Well, you of course, but..."

Esther had never really been deceived by Pomfret; she'd always deceived herself. Jane's revelations did not shock her. What upset her, what made the steel gleam in her eye was that Jane Holden had called him Charles, that a woman she could only see as servant, and a bad one at that, had once been on familiar terms with him.

"No buts, Charles. It's clear enough what Jack wanted. We need to think how we can carry out his wishes."

Evelyn ran over, knelt at her feet and embraced her. Nathanial came and sat by her, putting his arm round her shoulders. Pomfret spluttered, stuttered and stormed from the room.

Jane stood looking stunned and forlorn. Nobody noticed her. She faded imperceptibly from the room, like a ghost.

Chapter Thirty Eight

Field Marshall Haig had no very high opinion of the Pals battalions, the locally raised battalions such as the Lancashires. To him they had neither the training nor the experience, nor the elan for sophisticated tactics. Rush and cover, by means of which troops ran forward covered by their comrades whose fire kept the Germans heads down was, he deemed, beyond them. All that could be expected of them was that they would advance doggedly and steadily, carrying all the equipment necessary for them to dig in and hold any ground they gained.

When the time came for the British to play a major role, to take the initiative and launch a major offensive, Haig decided that an unprecedented bombardment of the German line would be necessary. It was essential for the German wire, the German dugouts and the German machine gunners to be blasted from their ridges and redoubts, if there was to be any hope of a breakthrough.

The bombardment lasted all through the hot days and nights of the last week of June. It was the longest and heaviest bombardment of the war. The howitzers, the 60 pounders, the 6", 8" and 12" guns roared and recoiled hour after hour, until their barrels were worn out and warped. The gunners stripped to the waist, their ears bleeding, choked by cordite fumes and blinded by smoke, loaded and fired, loaded and fired, loaded and fired, while the brass shell cases bounded and bounced all around them.

Officers with their field glasses observed the pounding of the enemy line hour after hour, day after day. They felt sorry for the destruction they wreaked. They felt pity for the defenders. Nothing could survive. Not a soul would be left when the British walked over, not even a solitary rat would be left alive.

On the eve of the offensive, before going into line, the Lancashires idling up a dusty track, fell in with a group of kilted Highlanders. Ben recognised one of them - Billy. But Billy did not recognise Ben. Although the bruises had gone, there was a lopsidedness to Ben's face and his nose was broken. Billy too showed signs of the toll war had taken. He was thinner, more haggard. He stared back aggressively and then sauntered over.

"What are you staring at you English bastard?"

"Billy, don't you recognise me? It's Ben."

Billy's face transformed at once from flint and granite under a threatening sky to become all sunshine and smiles.

"Ben! It's good to see you."

Ben introduced Yorky.

"Aye I mind him well. Here's my pals, Tom and Wally."

There was much handshaking and back-slapping, then they sat by the wayside and passed round cigarettes. It was a lovely evening. The distant banging of the guns was a familiar backdrop by now.

"What do you think of our chances, Billy?" Yorky asked.

"You're in trouble my friend. Things must be looking bad. I'll tell you for why. It's because we're here. They always bring in the 51st Highland Division when things are looking black. Isn't that so, lads?"

"Aye Billy, we were at Festubert and we were at Givenchy," said Willie.

"But all this shelling," Ben said. "There can't be a Fritz left alive."

"That's what they say, Ben," Billy said. "That's what those who won't be going over the top say, but I've been in one of them Jerry dugouts. Man, they're twenty feet down. I'm not saying they won't be getting a shaking, but they'll be there to greet us alright when we go over."

"Aye," said Willie, "and I've heard an officer say the wire's not cut."

"They're not using enough high explosive shells," Yorky said. "You can't cut wire with shrapnel. You might as well try and plait sand."

"Well we must keep our spirits up nevertheless and I wish we had some just now," Billy said.

"We have," said Yorky and produced his water bottle. "Ben gives me his ration, so I always have a drop by me." He passed it round.

Billy smacked his lips.

"It's no as good as whisky, but it'll do. Ben it's a thousand pities that you'll never taste a Highland malt."

"What part of the Highlands are you from?" Ben asked.

"Och you'll no have heard of it, a wee island called Cara."

Ben stared open-mouthed.

"My girl lives there."

Billy mirrored his astonishment. Ben explained.

"She's with her mother and aunt and the little lad at the big house. I can't remember what it's called."

"Achaglass," Billy said. "My mother wrote me about the bairn being born there. And you're the father?"

Ben shook his head, but was at a loss how to go on. Yorky put an arm round him.

"This lad is a hero. It was an officer got the poor lass in trouble and Ben finds him wounded in no man's land. He makes the officer promise to make an honest woman of her and carries him in on his back. Course the bastard goes back on his word and another officer takes all the credit and gets a medal. It should have been Ben who got that medal."

"That sounds about right," Willie said.

"I have a lassie myself, Ben," Billy said. "She's at the munitions in Glasgow just now. If there's a God in the world, one day the four of us will walk on the beach at Carraig Mor and watch the sun go down over the western isles. Man it's the rarest sight in all the world. I might even persuade you to taste a drop of Dew of Islay."

He held out his hand. Ben shook it. Both men had tears in their eyes.

At 7.00 on the morning of the attack, the bombardment intensified. Hundreds of thousands of shells of all calibres were sent over. It was no longer possible to single out an individual gun. They merged into a continuous roar, a deafening crescendo that could be heard in London. A man screaming in his comrades ear could not be heard. No new experience for many of the Lancashires, who had worked in the mills.

At 7.20 the mine at Hawthorn Ridge under the road to Beaumont Hamel was detonated. It was the climax to a prolonged and dreadful symphony. The ridge was flung thousands of feet into the air, blowing spotter planes off course and showering them with debris. The resulting crater was hundreds of feet in diameter. Further, smaller mines went off and then the barrage moved off the front line towards the German reserve positions.

When the early mist cleared, it was a fine morning. Every man carried over 60 pounds of equipment. Many had sandbags, shovels, picks, flares, flags, wire-cutters and cans of paint for marking captured guns, as well.

The front trenches were packed. They were like holiday-makers on the platform waiting for the holiday train. Ben kept adjusting his equipment to get a better balance. He was overburdened. He eyed the angle of the nearest trench ladder and knew it would take him all his strength just to climb out.

At 7.30 officers, dressed like the men so as not to be obvious targets, but carrying no equipment, climbed out, blowing their whistles and urging the men out.

By the time Ben got on the ladder, the German machine guns were chattering away. The dugouts had not been destroyed. The mines had been blown too early. The barrage had moved off the front line too soon. The Germans had plenty of time to emerge, set up their machine guns and begin to pour fire on the slowly advancing British.

Ben got out of the trench and began to slog forward. Men all round him were grunting and falling away as they were hit. Bullets tugged his sleeve. Bullets ripped up the ground at his feet. Bullets flew past his face. Ben kept going.

Many died queuing at the gap in the British wire. Many more died at the German wire that had not been cut. Soon there were more men lying on the ground than walking over it.

Still Ben went on. Still bullets avoided him, as though they'd no business with him. Was he immune? Was he being saved for Sadie?

He paused to resettle his equipment, but when he moved forward again, he walked into something. Something gave him a bad knock. Something shoved him back. Something made him stagger. The smoke and murk of no man's land obscured everything. He felt sick and dizzy. Could he go forward? Which way was forward? Where was he? And then he saw her.

There she was; Sadie. And he understood. He understood everything. Sadie waited for him by the unfurling edge of the sea, on the hard, wet sand that bore her scribbled reflection. She was examining her bare toes, then she looked sideways at him and smiled.

"Hello, Ben."

Ben had no burdens now, no equipment weighed him down. He too was barefoot. He walked over the sand towards her and it squirmed beneath his toes.

"I knew you'd be here," Ben said.

"And I knew you'd come," she replied.

She held out her hand and Ben took it. For the first time in many years, he was holding her hand. They walked together, splashing through the shallows. The water was warm. There was a breeze. That was warm too. The sky was blue with only the merest wisps of cloud. The sun was not quite at its zenith. The tide was on the ebb. All was bright, as though lit by an internal flame: the beach; the mountains; the forest; the brilliant sea; the far isles.

They walked on by the sea's edge, walked on around the bay, walked on to its far side, until they were the only two figures in the immensity of the bright, airy landscape, until they were so far away that even the keenest eye could not distinguish one from the other.